P9-BYA-052

The New York Times
Book of Needlepoint

THE NEW YORK TIMES
Book of

*Illustrations by Lisa Levitt
and Robert Cioran Crow*

Needlepoint

Elaine Slater

Quadrangle/*The New York Times Book Co.*

Copyright © 1973 by Quadrangle/The New York Times Book Co. All rights
reserved, including the right to reproduce this book or portions thereof
in any form. For information, address: Quadrangle/The New York Times
Book Co., 10 East 53rd Street, New York, New York 10022. Manufactured
in the United States of America. Published simultaneously in Canada by
Fitzhenry & Whiteside, Ltd., Toronto.

Library of Congress Catalog Card Number: 72-94654
International Standard Book Number: 0-8129-0339-0

Design by: BETTY BINNS

PHOTOGRAPHS: *Dennis Colwell of Toronto*
ASSISTANT ARTIST: *Rasa Skudra*
Cover needlepoint executed by Kathryn Currie.
Production by Planned Production

To my family with love

Acknowledgements

I wish to thank Mr. and Mrs. J. F. Barrett and Mr. and Mrs. Herbert Solway for their hospitality in loaning me the use of their lovely and gracious homes as settings for needlepoint.

I would also like to offer thanks to the Aggregation Gallery of Toronto for allowing me to photograph needlepoint in their striking art gallery.

And to Sophie Phillips—what would I have done without her patient typing and retyping of this manuscript?

And to Jo-An Baldwin and Mimi Hollenberg, whose suggestions were always good ones.

And to Dorothy Irwin whose great store of technical know-how combined with an unbelievably generous spirit helped solve the insoluble.

And to Kathy Currie who always found time to help.

And to Rosabel Levitt, upon whose impeccable taste in setting up photographs, and upon whose unselfish nature, I leaned so heavily. . . .

And to James Slater, my husband, who helped in every and any way, including learning needlepoint so that I might watch the workings of a leftie at first hand, and who stifled his irritation as his home became first a storage warehouse and then a photographic setting for needlepoint and yarns.

And to those who not only loaned me their lovely works of needlepoint, but delivered them to me and then picked them up at what had to be, at the very least, personal inconvenience, and who endured my repeated phone calls of reminder and request, I can only say thank you and thank you again for being the kind and exceptional people you are.

Batia Andrews, Laura Bader, Charlotte Bockner, Pat Bone, Eva Borins, Mary Bosley, Donia Brown, Eve Brummer, Elizabeth Bryce, Hillary Cohen, Barbara Cooper, Sally Croll, Kathryn Currie, Marjorie Edmund, Betsy Fee, Betty Gelman, Raylene Godell, Suzanne Goodman, Bee Gould, Charlotte Gustin, Florence Hacker, Doris Hancock, Dinnie Hatch, Barbara Ann Hynes, Mary Jukes, Pat Laing, Temmy Latner, Susan Levinsky, Susan Lind, Roberta Logie, Sheila Lubotta, Vikki Lyons, Nancy MacDonald, Marilyn Markovitz, Lynn McCullagh, Dorothy McKenzie, Sylvia Milrod, Sally Moore, Joan Moss, Eunice Mouckley, Phyllis Pepper, Barbara Roberts, Susan Robinette, Ruthe Rosenbaum, Joan Rosenthal, Carol Schipper, Margaret Scott-Atkinson, Pat Selby, Jackie Shulman, Abby Slater, Lisa Slater, Jim Slater, Janine Smith, Jo Stefaniuk, Lil Stein, Lillian Stupp, Catherine Sukerman, Celia Ungerman, Leena Visuri, Toni Wrightson and Connie Young.

My most sincere and grateful thanks.

Contents

Introduction, 1
What you will need, 5
Terms, 9
How to rule your canvas, 11

Lesson 1 The Brick Stitch
How to do the Brick Stitch 19
How, why and where to use the Brick Stitch 34

Lesson 2 Old Florentine Stitch
How to do the Old Florentine Stitch 41
How, why and where to use the Old Florentine Stitch 60

Lesson 3 The Parisian Stitch
How to do the Parisian Stitch 65
How, why and where to use the Parisian Stitch 79

Lesson 4 The Hungarian Point Stitch
How to do the Hungarian Point Stitch 85
How, why and where to use the Hungarian Point Stitch 102

Lesson 5 The Encroaching Upright Gobelin Stitch
How to do the Encroaching Upright Gobelin Stitch 107
How, why and where to use the Encroaching Upright Gobelin Stitch 114

Lesson 6 The Hungarian Ground Stitch
How to do the Hungarian Ground Stitch 119
How, why and where to use the Hungarian Ground Stitch 132

Lesson 7 The Upright Cross with Back Stitch
How to do the Upright Cross with Back Stitch 137
How, why and where to use the Upright Cross with Back Stitch 153

Lesson 8 The Mosaic Stitch

How to do the Mosaic Stitch 159
How, why and where to use the Mosaic Stitch 172

Lesson 9 The BNS or Basic Needlepoint Stitch

How to do the Basic Needlepoint Stitch 179

Lesson 10 The Continental pattern of the BNS

How to do the Continental pattern of the BNS 211

Lesson 11 The Whipped Flower

How to do the Whipped Flower 223

Blocking and Deciding, 228
The Alphabet, 235
Shopping Information, 248

Introduction

Why another book about needlepoint? Hasn't the subject been more than adequately covered in the spate of books issued recently?

The answer to that latter question is No!

In my needlepoint shop in Toronto, I have watched people struggle to learn from books. Each book is excellent in its own way. One describes, in sprightly and humorous tones and photographs, the trials and tribulations that went into each work, from original concept to completion. Another gives the history of needlepoint, includes beautiful examples of historic tapestries and chair seats, and names the stitches that were used. Yet a third shows how to design canvases, and a fourth has photographs and/or sketches of each of many stitches. But none of these books spares the reader and would-be needlepointer hours of trial and error, because a sketch or photograph of a few rows of stitches hardly covers the problems the new student faces.

In short, these needlepoint books have been written on the premise that the art can be mastered by a verbal discussion of its history, several diagrams and photos, and some very rudimentary text. The popular books on the subject, beautiful and informative as many of them are, have largely been written by people who are excellent needlepointers, but who are not currently engaged in teaching and are not, therefore, able to anticipate and hopefully forestall the usual errors and difficulties that face any beginner in a new area of expertise. The person who has been doing excellent needlepoint for years is unlikely to remember the rough spots, the beginner's errors and fears, whereas the teacher is reminded of them daily by her pupils.

What do you do about mistakes? What do you do at the end of a row or when you need a new strand of yarn? What do you do when you cannot complete a stitch because you have reached a border of some kind?

As a teacher of needlepoint, I know that it is not enough to describe a few stitches. One must try to anticipate the cries for help that issue from the needlepointer as he or she tries to undo a mistake or to avoid one. Realizing that there is a teaching gap that needs to be filled, I decided to take on the challenge and write a needlepoint book that does not mystify, confound, or intimidate by spreading the whole world of needlepoint before the beginner, but that starts at the beginning with a single, beautiful project, a sampler, and follows it through to completion. In this book I will show you how to work each stitch, warn you of the mistakes common to it, and go on to explain not only where it may be used on other canvases, but also how to use it, adapt it, and make it work.

We start with a sampler because it is precisely that—a "sampling" of nine or ten of the most useful and decorative of the hundreds of needlepoint stitches. When completed, your sampler will serve you in three important ways. Primarily it is the medium by which you will first learn the rudimentary art of working each stitch pattern. Then you can go on to experiment in various squares with the exciting possibilities of color and design.

Second, it serves as an important reference point to which you can return as you plan future projects, which may cover the entire range of needlepoint creations. It will serve to remind you not only of how you worked each stitch pattern, but more concretely, it will demonstrate how each stitch pattern may affect your project: Is it highly textured, or does it lie flat? Do you prefer it in one color, in highly contrasting colors, or in softly muted tones? Will it prove competitive with another design?

Last but not least, your sampler, in your own choice of colors, is a lovely and original work that you will treasure for its own sake.

My students have used their finished samplers not only as pillows for every conceivable spot in the house, but also framed for home or office, made into tote bags, or fitted to a chair or footstool. (See page 127.)

They have told me often that their samplers fit into their homes perfectly, regardless of whether the interiors are the most traditional or the most modern or unconventional. As an interior designer, I know that this is true. An exquisite Persian rug will be equally at home in an early American or Canadian setting, an elegant eighteenth-century European setting, or a contemporary redwood and glass setting. This relates to the profusion of colors set in a geometric form—precisely the qualities that we find in our samplers.

There is a story told of Knute Rockne, the famous Notre Dame football coach, who attempted to rally a faltering team during a half-time by beginning his pep talk with, "Gentlemen, let's start from the beginning! This is a football." In much the same manner, I would like to start by saying, "Ladies and Gentlemen, this is a needle" and, from this jumping-off point, assist you in the purchase of the proper canvas and yarn, in the selection of color, and even in your choice of needle.

I shall demonstrate each stitch pattern by means of newly evolved techniques developed in my own classes. As we proceed, we will stop frequently to provide solutions to those problems which my experience has shown to be the most likely to crop up. I will try

The sampler on the chair displays all needlepoint stitches while the patchwork cat and frogs on a blue background are worked in basic needlepoint stitch and Brick Stitch. The background for the dark green frog is done in Mosaic.

to anticipate the most common pitfalls and difficulties, recognizing that each needlepointer may have specific problems, and will use my accumulated experience with the beginner, as well as with the more experienced needleperson, to answer as many questions as possible.

It is anticipated that upon finishing the last page you will also be finishing a lovely needlepoint sample. By virtue of your experimentation with color and texture, which I encourage, each of your samplers will be unique. To my mind this is the most important aspect of creative needlepoint.

What you will need

In our classes we work our sampler on a 12-mesh white mono canvas. The 12-mesh canvas has 12 threads to the inch, both horizontally and vertically. Therefore, 12 of the basic small slanting needlepoint stitches going in any direction, north, south, east, or west, will cover a linear inch, and 12 times 12, or 144, of those same stitches will cover a square inch. We use the 12-mesh canvas because it is the most versatile, being large enough to work quite easily but small enough to get a good definition of design.

As you might imagine, a large mesh works best if you wish a striking, bold, and dramatic effect. It will not give you subtlety in shading if, for example, there are only 5 canvas threads to the inch, as there are in quickpoint canvas, but it is perfectly fine for bold or graphic designs. A canvas that is 18-mesh to the inch allows much exquisite color shading in each inch, but is harder to work as it is so fine. We have selected a happy medium, and for our own purposes the 12-mesh works out beautifully. But should you find that this mesh is still too fine for your eyesight, there is no reason not to use the 10 mesh, which is quite a bit larger but allows a lovely display of stitches. The finished pillow will be larger, about 15½

inches by 15½ inches instead of 13 inches by 13 inches. Remember that your canvas is never truly square, so all measurements must be approximate when dealing with needlepoint.

The mono canvas is a single thread canvas that looks like an ordinary window screen with evenly spaced vertical and horizontal threads. The other type of canvas generally available is called penelope (pen-EL-oh-pee), and it has double threads running in both directions. If possible, do not use the penelope canvas, as many of the decorative stitches will not cover it properly. If you cannot obtain mono canvas in your area, consult the back of this book for shopping information. The mono canvas costs about $3.50 for ½ a yard of high-quality linen or cotton canvas, and you can make two pillows or a multitude of smaller items from ½ a yard.

We use the white mono in our classes, but this is not of great importance. Some people find that the ecru or the greenish color is easier on the eyes. I personally prefer the white as I find that I can judge the effect of color juxtaposition better against a white background. In purchasing canvas, remember that its stiffness is your friend. Some people mistakenly look for soft canvas. Don't. It will slither off as you seek the holes and make every other stitch a game of hide and seek. Some of my pupils roll the canvas as they work it, or crumple it to get to the square they wish to work on. Rolling is preferable to crumpling, but neither is necessary. Just keep the canvas lying flat on your lap. The only hazard is that you will occasionally stitch right through and sew the canvas to your clothes. This is a nuisance that can be avoided by lifting the canvas a bit every stitch or so to be sure you haven't caught yourself. It can be funny when it happens, but not when it happens too often!

Your canvas will soften by itself in time, and there is nothing you can do about that, but do buy the best linen or cotton mesh and treat it kindly so that it will retain its stiffness as long as possible. When carrying it about, roll it neatly and hold it in place with your needle.

For the sampler you will require a piece of canvas 18 inches by 18 inches. (This is sufficient for 10- as well as 12-mesh.) One half yard of canvas will usually be enough for two pillows, as the canvas is generally about 36 inches wide. It is always best to leave an unworked area from 1½ inches to 2 inches wide all the way around the edge of your canvas to allow for later blocking and fabricating. If you have a sewing machine and are handy, work a zig-zag stitch around the edges of your canvas so that they will not fray and unravel. A strip of freezer or masking tape, or any heavy tape that is at least 1-inch wide, covering the edges will do as well.

In my classes, we use the "Persian" yarns exclusively. These yarns come in an enormous range of hues, from the most delicate to the most intense. Each strand is made up of three ply held together in such a way that they separate easily when necessary. This gives you great flexibility, as certain of the stitches look better and cover the canvas more fully when used in three ply; other stitches may appear too heavy or bulky in three ply, so merely peel off one ply before threading your needle. The Persian yarns have a beautiful texture as well as a special luminosity, but if you are not able to purchase them in your area, use any good tapestry wool or consult the shopping information at the back of the book. Knitting yarn is not suitable.

I find that each strand works best when cut to a length of about 24 inches. At this length, the yarn does not suffer from the excessive abrasion that occurs when it is pulled through the canvas too often.

Whatever tapestry yarn you decide upon, purchase about six ounces, or 250 yards if yarn is sold by the yard. The samplers are usually done either in a range of one color, from palest to most intense, five shades in all, or in three shades of one color and two of a complementary color, again five shades in all. If you decide upon the palest color as your background, you will have a muted effect. If you use the darkest color as your background, you will have a bolder and more dramatic effect. For purposes of clarity only, I use brilliant and contrasting colors in my graphs.

However, in selecting suitable colors for your own work consult the many samplers photographed in this book, and of course rely on your own color preferences as well as the requirements of the area in which it will be

Parts of a marvelous bird rug. After the birds are worked on 12-mesh canvas in BNS with a background of Brick Stitch, each is mounted on velvet and bound with ribbon.

used. Purchase about 2½ ounces or 100 yards of your background shade, and divide the other four colors according to your preference. For example, if you are using three pinks and two greens with pale pink as your background color, you might decide to divide your colors this way: 2½ ounces or 100 yards of pale pink, 1½ ounces or 60 yards each of medium pink and medium green, and ½ ounce or 20 yards each of dark pink and pale green. Notice that I am using the darkest pink and palest green as accent shades only, using more of the medium pink and green. But this is not mandatory. After buying the larger amount for your background shade, you might just as easily decide to divide the other four colors equally and purchase the same amount of each.

Our final requirement is a small but important one. You will need a tapestry needle. A size 18 is fine, but a size 20 will also do. The eye of a size 18 is a bit larger and it is easier to thread. As a general rule, size 18 is most convenient for a 10- or 12-mesh canvas. As your mesh size increases to a 14 or 16, your needle number would also increase to a 20 or 22.

Terms

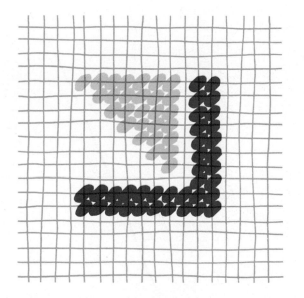

BNS

Basic Needlepoint Stitch. Continental and Basketweave mode.

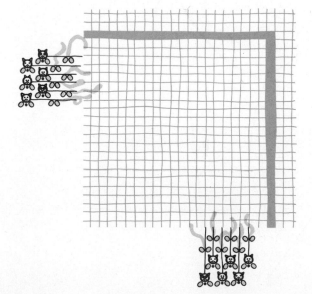

CATS

Canvas Threads which run from top to bottom of your canvas, to form the mesh.

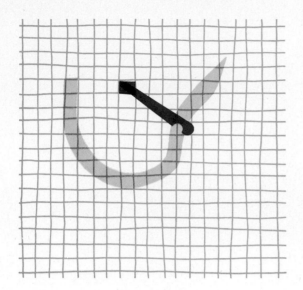

END HOLE
The hole through which your needle is inserted to the back of your canvas.

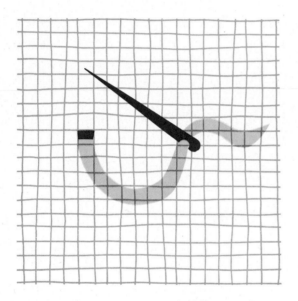

MAIN LINE HOLE
The hole through which your yarn and needle emerge to the front of your canvas.

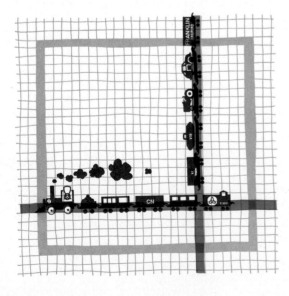

TRACK
A straight line of holes running across your canvas either from side to side or up and down.

How to rule your canvas

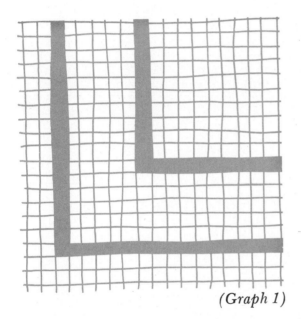

(Graph 1)

Since your canvas is blocked later by dampening it quite thoroughly, it is most important that you never use anything on it that is not completely waterproof. Many magic markers are said to be waterproof, but they blur and run when wet. This would ruin your sampler, so be absolutely sure when ruling to use only a good sharp pencil.

The process of ruling-in the squares is tedious but quite easy, being simply a matter of counting accurately. Accuracy is of the greatest importance, so work slowly and carefully, and check your count frequently. On an 18-inch by 18-inch piece of canvas, start about 1½ to 2 inches down from the top of the canvas and 1½ to 2 inches in from the left side. Pencil in, along a track between two threads, a horizontal and then a vertical line to form a corner. From this initial corner begin to count your canvas threads, following *graph 1* exactly. Be sure to count canvas *threads,* or CATS (see Terms), and not canvas *holes.* Your completed sampler will have 25 squares, each 24 by 24 canvas threads, surrounded by a border of six canvas threads *(graph 2)*. Your border around the sampler and around each of the squares will be six canvas threads wide; that is, your pencil lines will encompass six canvas threads before you begin to count your squares, which will

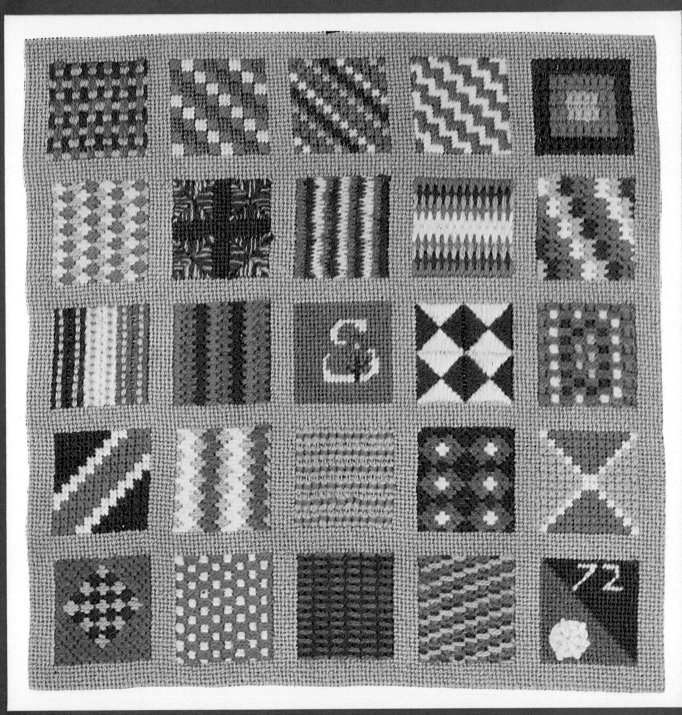

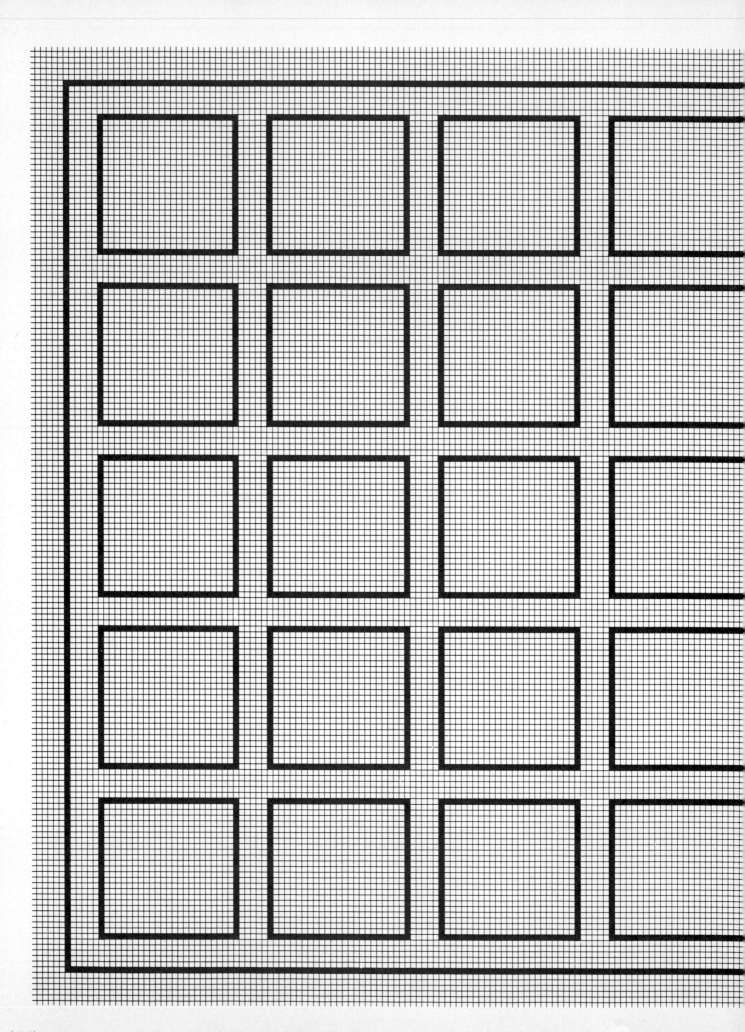

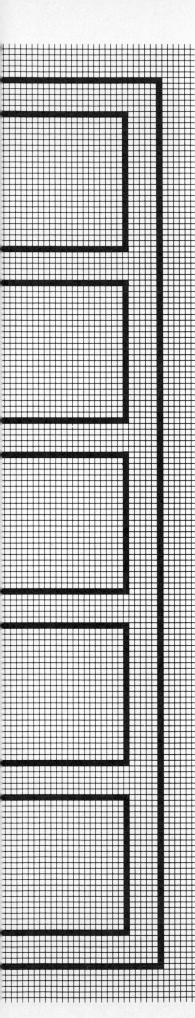

each encompass 24 canvas threads from top to bottom and side to side. Count carefully because a mistake at this stage will throw you off badly later on. All your pencil lines should be in the tracks between canvas threads, and not on the threads themselves.

It has been said that one picture is worth a thousand words, and this holds true here. Refer to your graph as often as you need to. Later, if one of your decorative stitches does not come out as I described it, your first thought after checking to see if your stitches look right, should be, "Did I count my square right? Have I 24 canvas threads running from top to bottom and from side to side?" Count again. If you are one thread off, your entire sampler will be off.

When your canvas has been ruled, you are ready to begin. Tie a bit of yarn in the center square to remind you not to use that square until later, when you will work your initial in it. Tie a bit of yarn in one of your corner squares also; it doesn't matter which corner, but exclude one corner square for the time being. It will be worked later in the basketweave, with a superimposed flower and the date. You will not do any of the decorative stitches in either of these two squares.

In working your first few squares, it does not matter what colors you decide to use, but by the time you are finished, you should have tried every possible color combination.

As you begin to fill in your sampler, try to achieve a balance in your use of color so that all your dark colors are not on one side or similar color combinations are not used repeatedly near one another. In selecting colors for various stitches, keep this balance in mind. You will use your background color in your squares, but use it somewhat

(Graph 2)

sparingly to be sure you have enough for your border.

One more word of caution. Many people, myself included, like to leaf through a book, stopping here and there, like a hummingbird in a summer garden, to sample the delights contained therein. However, it is suggested that this particular book be read in proper sequence, as one would a textbook, because the stitches are taught in a definite order, each leading on to the next in an orderly progression. And hints are given in each chapter in order to make the next chapter easier to follow. Thus, although the first stitch taught is in many ways the easiest, it is also given the most detailed treatment in an attempt to avoid, right from the start, any mistakes in comprehension. More is taken for granted in later chapters, as it is assumed that many of the most common errors will no longer prove troublesome. If you skip from here to there, you may miss many valuable tips that would make your work both easier and more beautiful. I would like to avoid as much as possible that poignant cry, "Where did I go wrong?"

The Brick Stitch

(Graph 1)

How to do the Brick Stitch

You will be using two colors for this square, so select a dark and a light yarn. In this chapter we have used blue for the dark and green for the light. It does not matter which two colors you select. I refer to them as a dark yarn and a light yarn for purposes of clarity. Begin by threading your needle with a dark yarn, using a full three ply of Persian. To thread a tapestry needle, hold it in your right hand, and with your left hand, loop the yarn tightly around the narrow end of your needle, keeping the loop very tight with your left thumbnail. Slide the loop up, over, and off the wider, or eye, end of your needle. Hold that thumbnail tightly in place, so that you have a tiny loop of yarn in your left hand. Force this loop through the eye of the needle. If you have not threaded a needle this way before, practice a few times; it becomes easier with each try *(graphs 1, 2, 3)*. Do not knot the yarn.

(Graph 2)

When I first began to teach, it never occurred to me that threading a needle might be a problem for some people. But it is indeed, and I do feel sorry for those pupils who have such a struggle in mastering this essential skill. Try to do it the correct way, but failing that, do it any way you can or buy a needle with the largest eye possible.

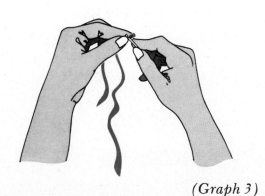

Keeping the canvas flat on your lap, pull the needle up from the back of the canvas to the front, exactly in the lower left-hand corner of the square you have chosen to work. Remember, you are saving your center square and one corner square for special treatment later.

(Graph 3)

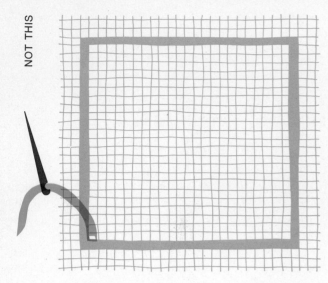

The pencil lines that form each square are considered a part of that square, so be sure that you have come up to the front of your canvas right *on* the pencil line at the juncture of your left pencil line and the bottom pencil line (NOT THIS *graph 4*, BUT THIS *graph 5*).

(Graph 4)

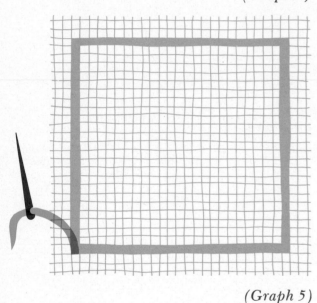

Leave about 1 inch of yarn in the back of your canvas with your first stitch, and hold this little tail of yarn in such a way that with your following stitches you can cover it, stitch over it, and anchor it. This is important as you do not want to lose your stitches later on because your initial stitch was not anchored properly.

(Graph 5)

*These lovely floral canvases with Brick Stitch
backgrounds represent the 12 provinces of Canada.
See plate on page 71 for detail.*

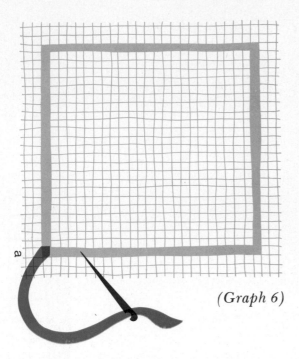

Now, moving straight to your right along the bottom pencil line, insert your needle past four up-and-down vertical canvas threads, or CATS *(graph 6)*. Study this graph carefully as a great many of the decorative stitches that we will be learning cover these same four up-and-down vertical CATS, as I shall refer to them. So become accustomed to this configuration as rapidly as possible.

(Graph 6)

Some stitchers will always carefully count those four vertical CATS with each stitch. This is slow but sure. Others gain the facility to see at a glance that four CATS covered is the same as encompassing three empty holes *(graph 7)*. This is quicker, but it may lead to an occasional careless mistake.

Insert your needle through to the back of your canvas, four CATS to the right, along the bottom pencil line (be sure you are right on the pencil line).

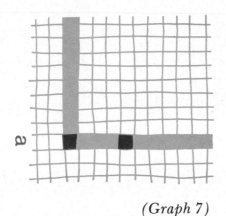

(Graph 7)

In the same motion, skip track B and bring your needle once again to the front of your canvas, emerging on the left-hand pencil line on track C *(graph 8)*.

From this position once again move straight to your right, covering four CATS, insert your needle, and in the same motion, emerge again on your left-hand pencil line two tracks up on track E *(graph 9)*.

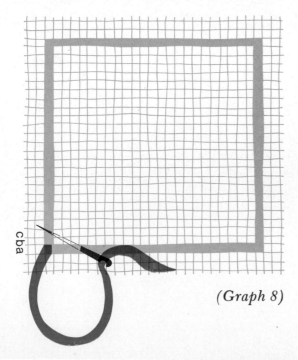

(Graph 8)

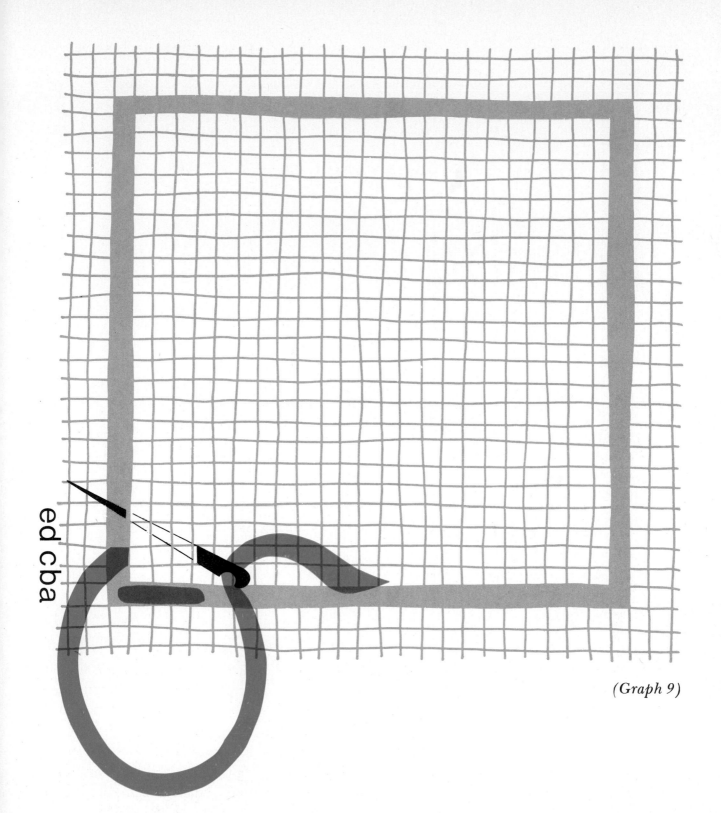

ed cba

(Graph 9)

(Graph 10)

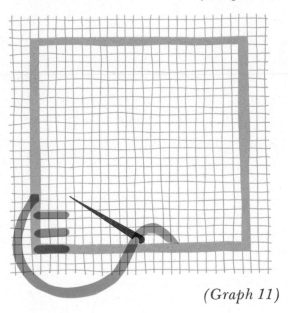

(Graph 11)

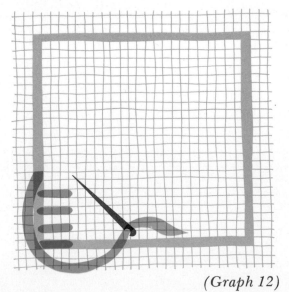

(Graph 12)

Be sure that your stitches are not slanting, but are running straight across each track (NOT THIS *graph 10,* BUT THIS *graph 11*). Repeat this pattern right up to and including your final stitch of this row which is on the top pencil line *(graphs 12, 13, 14, 15).*

After you have inserted your needle on the pencil line, pull your yarn through to the back of the canvas, and turning your canvas over so that the back side faces you, weave your needle under the last two stitches on the back to anchor your yarn. Turn your canvas so that the right side is facing you again, and pull your needle through to the front of your canvas in any free area nearby, leaving this excess yarn hanging there until you need to use it again *(graph 15).* It may seem strange that I suggest that you pull your yarn to the front of your canvas in this manner, but there is a sound reason for it. If you were to leave this tail dangling down in the back until you were ready to use it again, it would almost certainly become tangled in your next stitches, and not only would it become totally unusable, but it would mat the back of your canvas, making it lumpy and unsightly. On the other hand, if your yarn is waiting for you on the front of your canvas where you can see it, it is much less likely to become entangled in anything. Some people prefer to keep their needle on this waiting strand and use another needle for their next color. This is perfectly all right. I have no trouble threading tapestry needles, so I usually slip them off and rethread with each new strand.

Take a good look at the row you have just completed. Are all your stitches even, or have you accidentally made one shorter or longer than the others? Each must cover four CATS. If you have inadvertently worked a three-CAT or five-CAT stitch, you should be able to see your mistake fairly quickly, as your stitches will look varied in size.

If you find you have made a mistake a short way

(Graph 13)

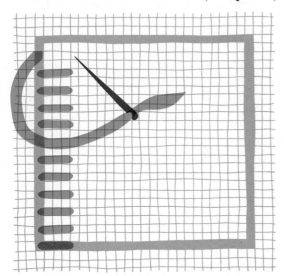

(Graph 14)

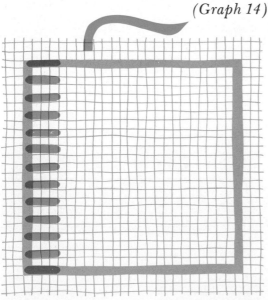

(Graph 15)

back, pull out your stitches to one stitch *prior* to your mistake, if you can, and begin again. If you cannot pull out the stitches because the yarn has become anchored along the way, or if your mistake is too far back to warrant so much additional pulling and abrasion on the strand, you must cut out the stitches, but be careful not to cut your canvas. Use sharply pointed small scissors to cut back to your mistake, and then pull out a few additional stitches and use this bit of yarn to anchor your previous stitches. That is, just thread up with the end of your cut yarn and weave it in and out the back before commencing again with your new strand.

For the lazybones and the not so meticulous among you (and I am sometimes to be counted in this group), it is often perfectly acceptable, if you worked a stitch that is too short, to work another right over it in the proper length. As many of these decorative stitches are quite bulky anyway, no one will notice. But don't try it on flat stitches such as the mosaic or your basic needlepoint stitch (BNS). Here you must rip.

If you DO cut your canvas—and, alas, I am often called upon to repair the over-zealousness of my pupils—place a small square of matching canvas behind the tear and work your stitches through double mesh for three or four rows all around the tear. It's not as easy as it sounds, so it's best to avoid this error if possible.

If you have done the square correctly (always assuming that you have counted and ruled out your square properly so that it has exactly 24 canvas threads between your top and bottom lines), you should have ended this row with a stitch exactly on the top pencil line. Sometimes when you do not end in this manner, it means that you forgot to skip a track somewhere along the line, or perhaps you slanted a stitch instead of having each stitch go perfectly straight from left to right across your

NOT THIS

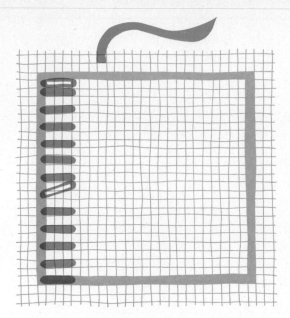

(Graph 16)

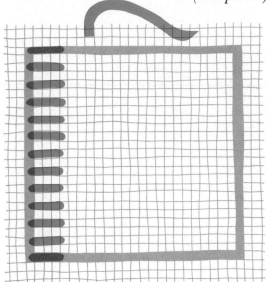

(Graph 17)

canvas (NOT THIS *graph 16,* BUT THIS *graph 17*). If you have ended wrong and cannot find the mistake, you must count your threads in the square again, as the mistake will most probably be in the counting.

A word about your tension. I am not referring here to the state of your nerves at learning a new skill, but rather to the tension placed upon your stitches. You should be pulling your yarn tightly enough so that you feel it touch the canvas firmly, but not so tightly that it pulls the canvas out of shape even the slightest bit. It has been my experience that students are more likely to have their stitches too loose and loopy and disordered looking than to have them pulled too tight. Either extreme is bad, of course. Try for the happy medium, which is a fluffy textured look that is even, with no shaggy or sloppy surfaces, and no tightly pulled, thin stitches that stretch the canvas out of shape.

You are ready for your second row of the Brick Stitch. Thread your needle with the light-colored yarn, again three ply if you are using the Persian yarn, and bring your needle through to the front of your canvas on track B, *not* on the left-hand pencil line, but two CATS to the right of it. This is just above the center of your first stitch of the previous row *(graph 18).* Once again, leave about 1 inch of yarn in the back of your canvas, holding this tail in such a way that your next stitches will cover, splice, and anchor it.

Bring the yarn across the canvas to your right, perfectly straight along track B, and insert your needle four CATS over. Since you began this stitch two CATS to the right of your previous row of stitches, it also ends two CATS to the right of your previous row.

In the same motion, bring your needle to the front of the canvas again, skipping to track D, two CATS in from the pencil line *(graph 19).*

26

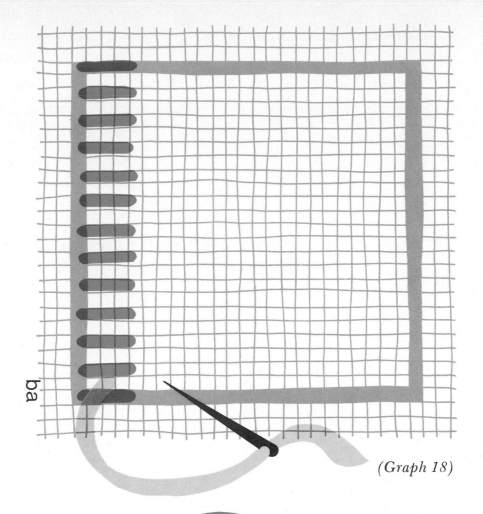

ba

(Graph 18)

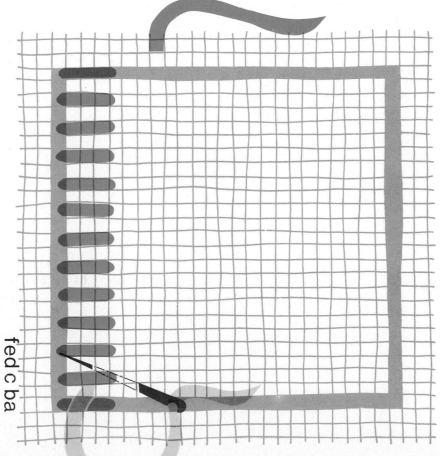

fed c ba

(Graph 19)   27

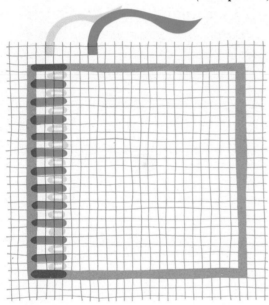

(Graph 20)

Again, work a four-CAT stitch, emerging in one motion on track F, prepared to work yet another four-CAT stitch, and so on.

As you continue up your square in this pattern, you may begin to see why this has been called the Brick Stitch pattern. Each stitch starts midway above the previous stitch, always leaving a jagged edge, in the same manner as that in which bricks are laid. If you find you are getting a straight edge, you are making a mistake somewhere. You are either not beginning in the proper place or you are not making your stitches in the proper length of four CATS (NOT THIS *graph 20,* NOR THIS *graph 21,* BUT THIS *graph 22*).

(Graph 21)

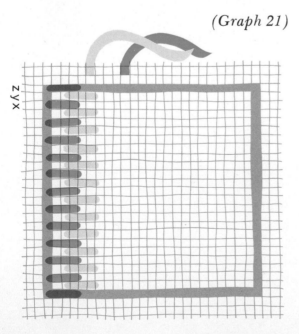

(Graph 22)

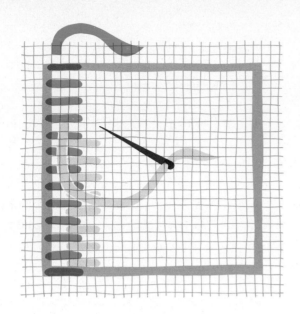

Continue up your square with your light-colored yarn. You will work your last stitch on track Y (see graph), as you must never go beyond the pencil line border of your square *(graphs 23, 24)*. Pull your needle through to the back, turn your canvas over again so that the back side faces you, and weave your yarn under the last two stitches on the back in order to anchor your yarn.

(Graph 23)

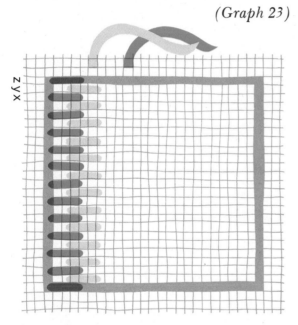

Now bring your leftover strand to the front of the canvas in a nearby free area as you did before *(graph 24)*.

(Graph 24)

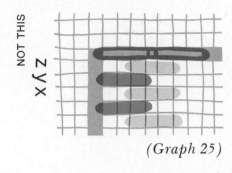

(Graph 25)

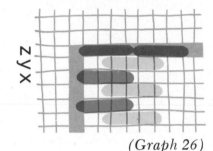

(Graph 26)

Your dark yarn has been waiting for you at the top of your canvas. Pull it through to the back and thread your needle. (If you left a needle threaded on the dark strand, simply pull it through its hole to the back of the canvas.) Emerge at the front of your canvas on track Z, sharing a hole with the dark stitch already completed on that track. In needlepoint you will always be sharing each hole so that the canvas will not show through, but be careful not to split the thread of the stitch already in the hole, as that would give your work a furry, sloppy appearance (NOT THIS *graph 25*, BUT THIS *graph 26*).

Once again, in the same pattern as before, but now working from top to bottom, move straight to the right, cover four CATS, and emerge in the same motion, sharing a hole two tracks down on track X. I make a point of urging you to end one stitch and begin the next in a single motion for several reasons. The first is simply speed of execution. If you pull your needle through to the back with each stitch, you slow yourself down enormously. But there is another disadvantage which may even be more important: if you continually pull your needle all the way through to the back, as some people are tempted to do, you lose the rhythm of the stitch. You are doing one stitch at a time instead of a *pattern* of stitches, and this will set you back a great deal in terms of understanding the mechanics of the stitch, as well as in speed and efficiency. Some of my students have difficulty with this at first as they may have become accustomed to completing one stitch at a time. I always urge them to make this special effort right at the beginning as it is worthwhile in the long run.

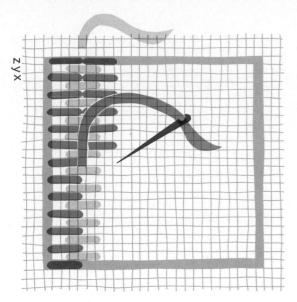

(Graph 27)

Work your way down the square with your dark yarn *(graph 27)*. If you find you are running out of yarn, do not let the end get too short. Everyone, including myself, has the inclination to try to stretch that last little bit of yarn just one more stitch, but don't be tempted to do this. When your yarn end is just a bit longer than the length of your needle, it is time to pull it all the way through to the back of your canvas and weave the leftover tail of yarn in and out of the stitches, being careful, of course, not to let it show through on the front. Snip off the remaining end close to the surface so that you have a nice neat back. Then thread up again with a new strand of the same color yarn.

You have the option now of either starting this new strand by weaving it in and out of the back stitches prior to coming forward on the canvas. Or you can do as we did with the very first stitch and leave a little 1-inch tail in the back and hold it in such a way that you cover and anchor it with your subsequent stitches. It really doesn't matter which method you use with your later rows, as the final effect is the same. Bring the new strand of yarn forward to the front of your canvas, sharing a hole as the pattern indicates.

At the end of each row of the Brick Stitch pattern, you must weave your yarn under the last two stitches at the back, and then be sure to pull your leftover yarn through to the front to wait for you. Finish your square in the pattern thus begun, noting that all your dark stitches share holes with dark stitches, and your light stitches share holes with light stitches.

When you have reached the far right pencil line, you will be left with a jagged edge on both sides of your square. On each side, your dark yarn extends to the pencil line, but the light yarn misses by two CATS.

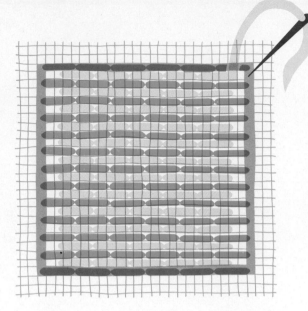

(Graph 28)

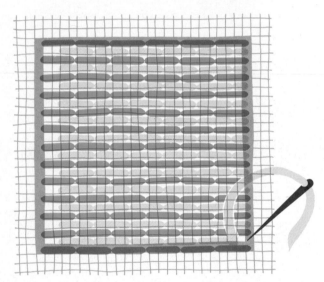

(Graph 29)

Since we want to have a straight edge running around each square and not have bare canvas showing, we must adapt our remaining stitches so that they cover the bare canvas, giving us a straight line, but at the same time they must not disrupt the basic pattern of the stitch. These adapting, or "compensating," stitches are really quite easy with the Brick pattern, but they are nonetheless very important. You will discover more about the use and necessity of compensating stitches in the section on How, Why, and Where To Use the Brick Stitch.

As has been noted above, your light yarn shares a hole with light yarn, and as it is the light rows that are incomplete, we must now work with the light yarn. It is not important whether you start from the top or from the bottom as long as you remember to share a hole with the proper stitch as you go along. If you have yarn waiting for you at the top of your canvas, you might as well start there.

Working on the right side first, come through to the front of the canvas, sharing a hole with your first light-colored stitch, and then move straight to your right only two CATS (the pencil line boundary will not permit you to go further), insert your needle, and come forward again in the same motion, sharing a hole with your next light color stitch two tracks away.

Continue to make these two-CAT stitches up or down your canvas to give you a straight edge *(graphs 28, 29)*. When you are finished, pull your needle through to the back, weave the yarn under, and snip it off as you will not be needing it any more.

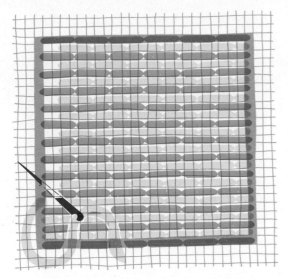

(Graph 30)

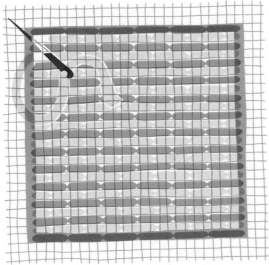

(Graph 31)

Now finish the left-hand side of the square in the same manner. It is probably already clear to you that you come to the front of the canvas with your light yarn, on the left-hand pencil line, and bring your needle over two CATS to share a hole with the light-colored stitch, and again in one motion, come through to the front on the pencil line two tracks away *(graphs 30, 31)*.

The important fact to remember here is that the Brick Stitch pattern is made up of four-CAT stitches, *but* when you cannot make a four-CAT stitch because of a boundary of some sort, you simply adapt to circumstances and make whatever length stitch you *can* make short of four CATS. This knowledge will be important later if you decide to use this versatile stitch for a background.

When you have finished this final row, pull your yarn through to the back, weave it under, and snip off. Your first square is completed!

If you have any strands of yarn still waiting for you at the front of the canvas, pull them through to the back, weave, and snip.

You have done this first square in two colors, a dark and a light. I asked you to do this for ease of teaching, but now that you have mastered this stitch, experiment with color. You might try using several colors, from dark to light, one row after another. Or, if you feel confident enough, you might do every other stitch in an alternate color, or even a series of colors. You will be amazed at what diverse patterns emerge and how different the stitch appears in different colors. Once you have the rhythm of the stitch, give your imagination free rein.

You can also vary your sampler by simply giving your canvas a quarter turn, so that the upper right-hand corner now becomes your lower right-hand corner. The stitches of your first square then seem to be moving up and down instead of left to right, a change of direction that will lend more variety and interest to your sampler. In fact, in many of your later designs when you use the Brick Stitch pattern (this is particularly true with Bargello), you may prefer the up and down configuration that a quarter turn of your canvas gives you. Some teachers teach this stitch in an up and down fashion, but I believe it is much easier to learn and less awkward to do when worked from left to right as we have done.

Do one additional square of your sampler in the Brick Stitch pattern in your own choice of colors. Don't work this additional square right next to the one you have just completed as you will want your sampler to have a balanced appearance. This does not mean that it should be completely symmetrical, but you would not want identical stitches, or identical color combinations, side by side.

How, why and where to use the Brick Stitch

Once I received a call from a woman who urgently requested private lessons because she was in the midst of a pregnancy with complications and expected that at any time she might have to go to the hospital for an extended period. She was most anxious to learn as much as possible so that she could while away the hospital hours with needlepoint. In that first hour I taught her the Brick Stitch pattern and several forms of the basic needlepoint stitch, or BNS, which is used for the border. She left her lesson to dash off to a doctor's appointment and entered the hospital the very same day. Six weeks later she proudly brought in her completed sampler—all 25 squares done in the Brick Stitch!

This was carrying a good thing a bit too far.

Now that you have mastered the Brick Stitch pattern, you probably wonder what you should do with it? How should you use it? Why the Brick Stitch and not another decorative stitch? Where does it show off to its best advantage as opposed to some of the other stitches?

The greatest virtue of the Brick Stitch pattern is that it is quick and easy to do. It is very flexible and can easily be miniaturized or enlarged, covering any even number of CATS, for instance, two CATS for a smaller stitch or six CATS for a larger one. It compensates easily since the pattern is quite uncomplicated, and this also makes it an excellent background stitch as it does not try to steal the limelight from your central design.

The Brick Stitch pattern will cover a large area in less than half the time it would take if the basic small slanted needlepoint stitch were used. On a 12-mesh canvas there are 144 basic needlepoint stitches to the square inch, but only about 65 Brick Stitches to the same area. If you multiply that difference by the number of square inches to be covered on an average canvas, you will realize what an enormous saving this is in time and energy.

But if time saving were the only advantage and the Brick Stitch added nothing, or perhaps even detracted from your design, there would be no point in using it. But this is not the case. By using the Brick Stitch in one color only as a background, you actually bring to your canvas a three-dimensional effect that sets your basic needlepoint work into relief and has a most pleasing look.

The fact that the Brick Stitch compensates quite easily without muddying your basic stitch pattern too much is also a great advantage. When you use it as a background stitch, you will have to work around your central design, the outline of which may be extremely uneven, and ease of compensating is important.

The Brick pattern is also the basis for all Bargello (pronounced Bar-jello) stitchery and can be used to form a limitless number of designs. Bargello is an ancient form of needlepoint, thought to have originated in Florence, Italy, many centuries ago. Although it has many beautiful permutations, it is basically the Brick Stitch with colors utilized to form an endless variety of repeated patterns.

Because it is really so uncomplicated, the Brick Stitch does best when used in either of two diametrically opposite ways. The first is as a background stitch used in only one color. Worked in this manner it affords a lightly textured, non-competitive, rapid working, easily compensated, three-dimensional effect. Its only drawback is that it is quite a large stitch and might prove on 12-mesh canvas to be too loopy or loose for a rug, chair seat, or eyeglass case, items that receive a great deal of use or abuse. The remedy is to use 14-, 16-, or 18-mesh, so that the stitches become smaller. Or you might miniaturize the pattern so that each stitch will cover only two CATS. But 12-mesh would be adequate for a pillow or wall hanging, or even for a skirt hem or cuffs.

The other way in which the Brick Stitch pattern is most exquisite is in the Bargello mode. This simple stitch pattern easily adapts so that it forms an endless array of geometric, repeated patterns which stand completely on their own when used with a multitude of softly shaded colors. Here, too, it is best to use 14-, 16-, or 18-mesh canvas on items that will receive much use.

Although the Brick Stitch is the first stitch taught because in many ways it is the least complex, I believe you will find, as I have, that it is perhaps the single most useful decorative stitch, so don't slight it. It deserves your careful attention.

For many imaginative and effective uses of the Brick Stitch, refer to pages 3, 7, 71, 92, 113, 127, 173, 182, 195, and 229.

Old Florentine Stitch

How to do the Old Florentine Stitch

If you have completed your work for Lesson One, you have finished two squares in the Brick Stitch pattern. Remember, you are saving your center square and one corner square for later use.

With your sampler flat on your lap, thread your needle with a light yarn in the full three ply of Persian. We will use just two colors for this first square in the Old Florentine stitch, but I hope you will experiment later with color. In this chapter we have used green for the light and pink for the darker.

For now, select a free square; with the exception of the two squares noted above, it does not matter which square you choose. When you have more squares filled, you can try to achieve a balance in color and stitchery, but for the time being, just don't place your Brick square next to another Brick square, or an Old Florentine square next to another of the same type.

Pull your needle up from the back of the canvas to the front at the juncture of the two pencil lines in the lower left hand corner. Remember, your first stitch should always be right on the pencil line. (Refer to your Brick Stitch *graphs 4 and 5.*)

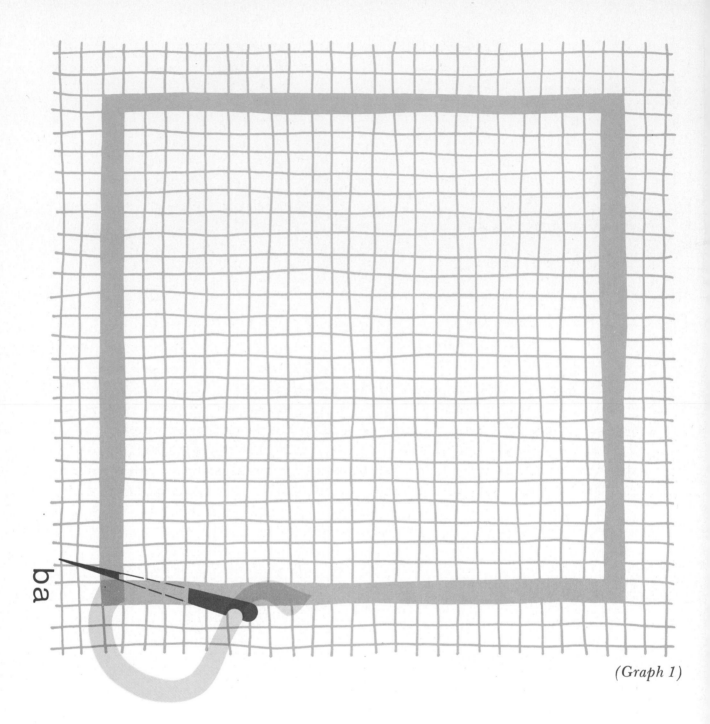

(Graph 1)

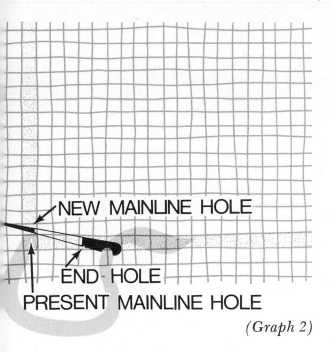

NEW MAINLINE HOLE

END HOLE

PRESENT MAINLINE HOLE

(Graph 2)

Pull your yarn straight to the right, across four vertical canvas threads, or CATS, as you did before, insert your needle, and in the same motion emerge on the left-hand pencil line, *but* on the very next track this time, track B *(graph 1).*
Be sure to insert your needle and emerge on the front of your canvas again in the same motion. If you take the time to pull your yarn all the way through to the back before beginning your next stitch, you will not only be slowed down considerably, but will also very likely lose the rhythm of the stitch, as I have said before.
Note that every time you pull your needle through to the front of the canvas, in what we will call the Main Line Hole (see Terms), you are *beginning* a stitch. And every time you insert your needle, you are *finishing,* or *completing,* a stitch in what is called the End Hole (see Terms). So each stitch has two parts: a beginning and an end. Or rather, an end and a beginning in one motion *(graph 2).* I suggest that you end one stitch and begin the next in a single motion because if you do lose your place, you'll find yourself poking through from the back to find the correct hole.

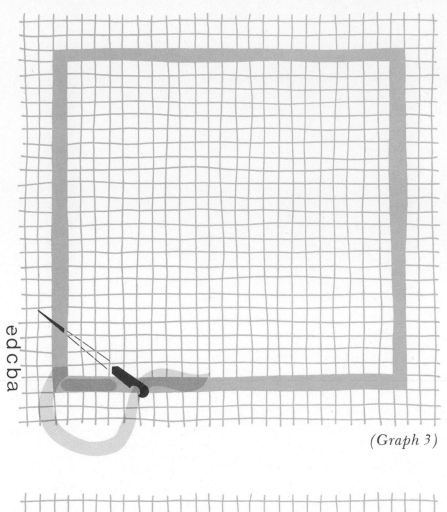

edcba

(Graph 3)

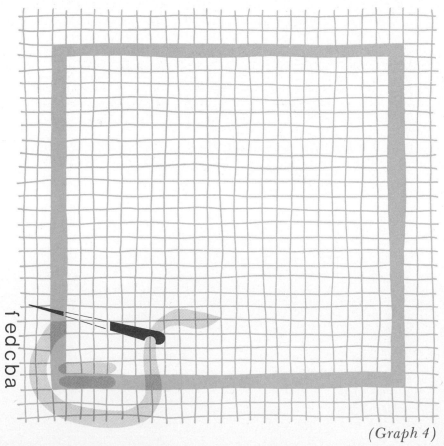

f'edcba

(Graph 4)

44

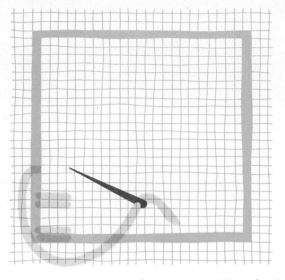

(Graph 5)

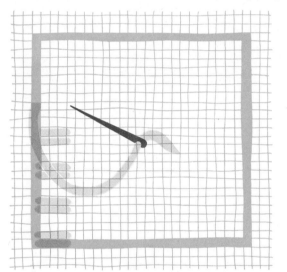

(Graph 6)

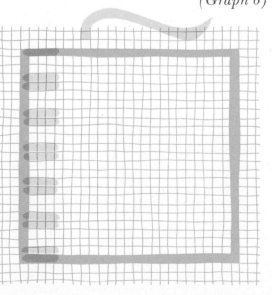

(Graph 7)

This repetition of instructions may slow you down a bit, but I have found that it is very valuable to emphasize and reemphasize certain points of great importance. With each repetition I will try to add an additional hint or concept so that it will not be a complete waste of time for those of you who have mastered the original instructions.

Now, you have worked one four-CAT stitch along the bottom pencil line and emerged on the left-hand pencil line on track B. Insert your needle once again across four CATS to the right so that you have two identical four-CAT stitches, one right above the other.

Now *skip* two tracks and emerge at track E on the left-hand pencil line *(graph 3)*. Once again bring your needle straight to the right across four CATS on track E, emerging on track F at the left-hand pencil line.

Work a second four-CAT stitch paralleling the first, and then *skip* two tracks and repeat the pattern *(graph 4)*.

Continue in this manner, working two parallel stitches and then skipping two tracks before working another two parallel stitches *(graphs 5, 6, 7)*.

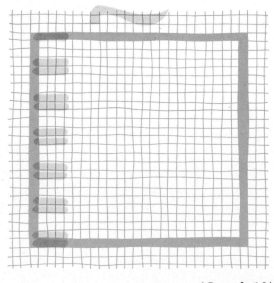

If you are working the square correctly (and assuming that you counted correctly in the first place, that is, 24 by 24 canvas threads), you will find that you end up at the top of your square with a *single* four-CAT stitch. Remember to work that last single stitch on the top pencil line. Despite your pattern, the borders of your square form an absolute boundary that you must never cross. Therefore you must not work that second parallel stitch (NOT THIS *graph 8,* NOR THIS *graph 9,* BUT THIS *graph 10*). *Do not* let your remaining yarn dangle at the back of your canvas. Pull it through somewhere nearby on the front to wait to be used again *(graph 10).*

(Graph 8)

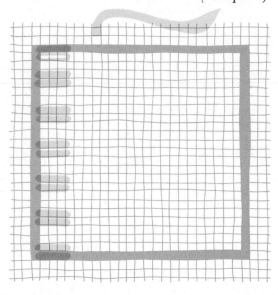

(Graph 9)

(Graph 10)

Miniature secretary holds jewel case worked in Flat Stitch, an enlarged form of Mosaic—initials in BNS. Eyeglass case beside it has BNS flowers surrounded by Old Florentine. Next eyeglass case is done in Oblong Cross with Backstitch. Purse has Hungarian Ground background while scissors case uses Hungarian Point. Mini-sampler has a Mini-Brick, Hungarian Ground and Upright Cross with Backstitch. Eyeglass case in Flat Stitch and pincushion worked in variation of Hungarian Point.

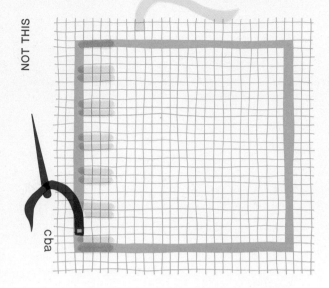

(Graph 11)

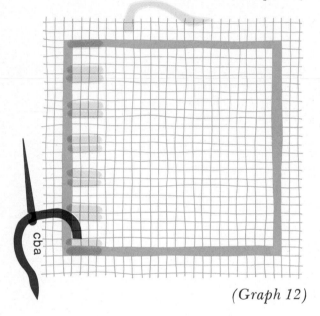

(Graph 12)

For your second row, thread up with your darker color. Start from the back of the canvas, bring your needle forward to the front on the first empty track, track C, *one* CAT to the right of the pencil line.

In this row of stitches you do *not* come up *on* the left-hand pencil line, but one CAT in (NOT THIS *graph 11,* BUT THIS *graph 12*).

Insert your needle across two CATS to the right on track C, and emerge again on the front of your canvas, one track above on track D, again one CAT to the right of the pencil line (*graph 13*).

Work another small two-CAT stitch straight to the right and skip two tracks, emerging on track G, one CAT in from the pencil line (*graph 14*).

You will notice that these small stitches sit midway between your two parallel larger stitches. They do not begin on the left-hand pencil line where the larger stitches begin, nor do they extend as far. They are one CAT smaller at each end.

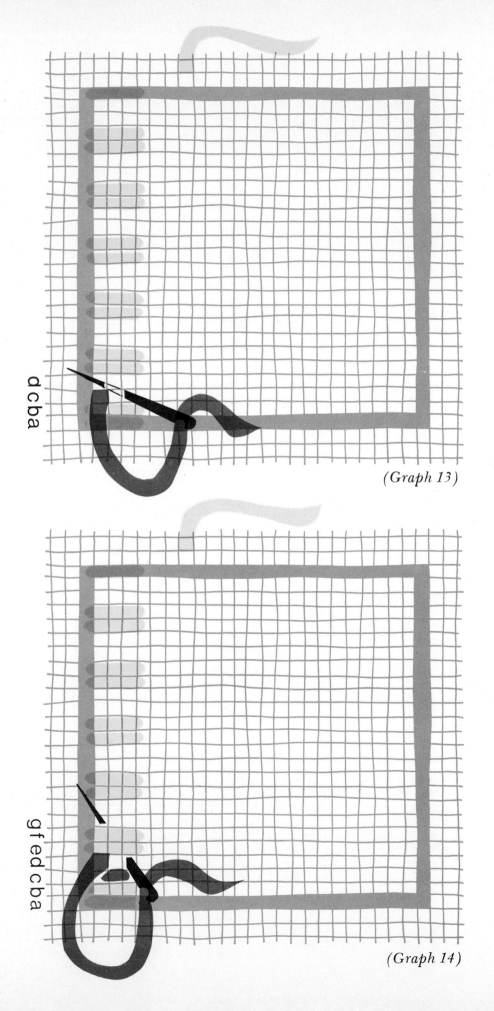

dcba

(Graph 13)

gf ed cba

(Graph 14)

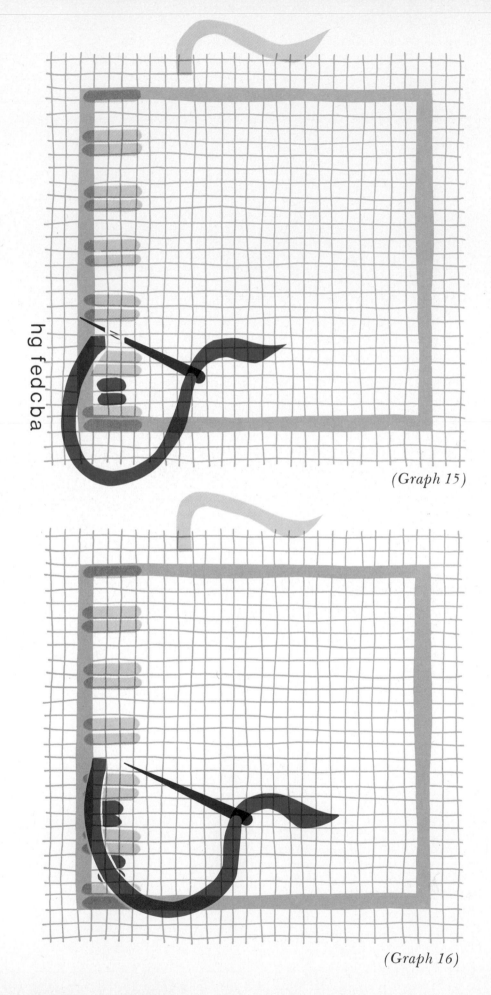

hg fedcba

(Graph 15)

(Graph 16)

50

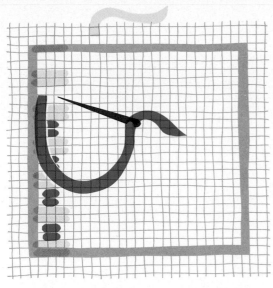

(Graph 17)

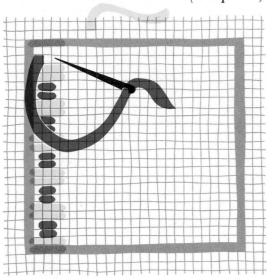

(Graph 18)

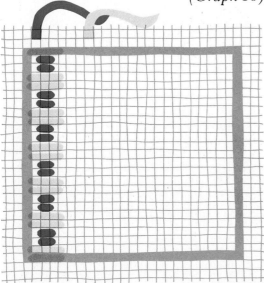

(Graph 19)

Run your needle across track G, cover two CATS, insert, and emerge on track H *(graph 15)*. Work your second two-CAT stitch, and skip the next two tracks, which already have the larger stitches on them.

Continue this pattern as far as you can, ending with two small stitches, and once again pull your leftover yarn forward on the canvas in some free spot nearby to wait for you as you did before *(graphs 16, 17, 18, 19)*.

Now, if you have your original light yarn waiting for you, pull the strand through to the back and thread up. (If you do not have yarn waiting, simply start with a new strand of light yarn.) We shall work from the top to the bottom of the square this time.

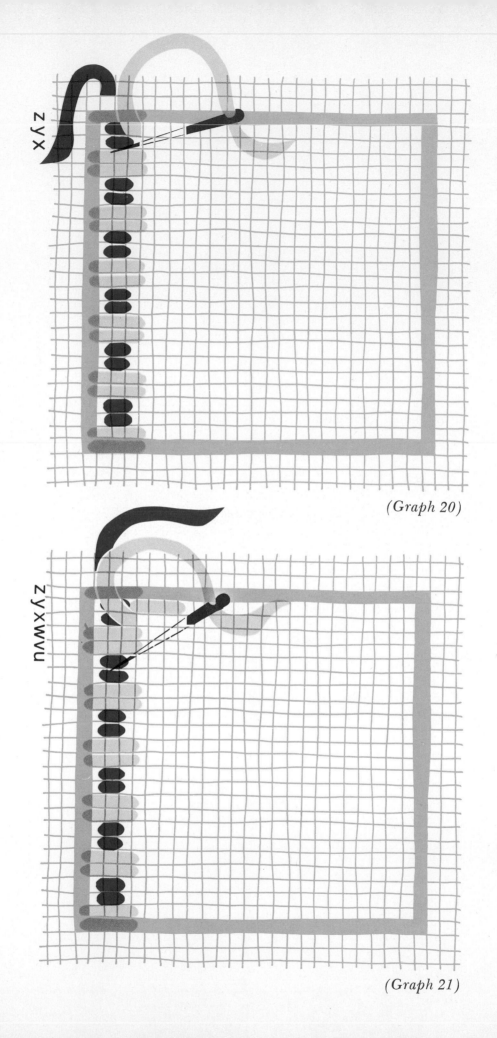

(Graph 20)

(Graph 21)

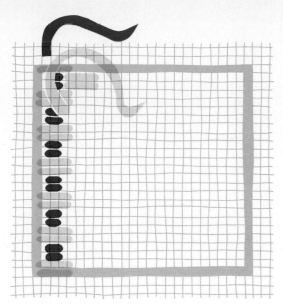

(Graph 22)

Pull your needle through to the front of your canvas, *sharing a hole* with your topmost little dark stitch.

Bring your needle straight to the right on this track, cover four CATS, and emerge in one motion immediately below on track X, sharing a hole with the next small stitch *(graph 20)*.

Once again, work a four-CAT stitch straight to the right. Now run your needle down the back of your canvas, skipping two rows, emerge at track U, and share a hole *(graph 21)*.

Work a four-CAT stitch and come forward on the canvas immediately below on track T *(graph 22)*.

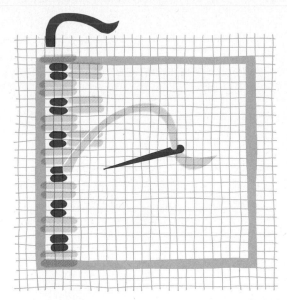

(Graph 23)

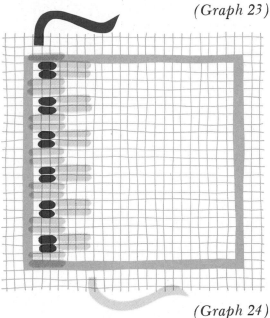

(Graph 24)

Continue down your square in this manner, working a pair of parallel light-colored stitches, each four CATS long, nestling right up against and sharing a hole with the small two-CAT dark stitches *(graphs 23, 24)*.

Once again, remember that when you find you are running out of yarn, don't let that final little end get too small or it will be hard to weave through the back. Keep it larger than the length of your needle so you can maneuver it, and your final stitches will not look pinched and twisted. When you see that it is time for a new strand, pull your needle through to the back and weave the tail of leftover yarn in and out, being sure that it doesn't show through to the front. Snip off the end and start with a new strand.

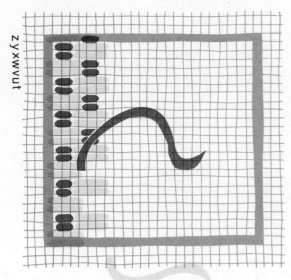

(Graph 25)

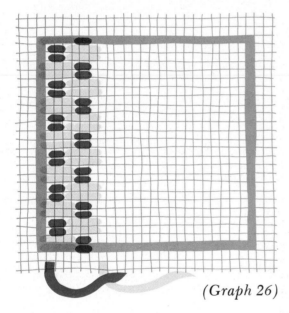

(Graph 26)

Now begin the fourth row. Thread up with the dark color waiting for you at the top. It is always possible to work these stitches either from top to bottom or bottom to top. The direction I work is dictated solely by where I have leftover yarn waiting for me.

Pull your yarn through to the front on the top pencil line, sharing a hole with the single light-colored four-CAT stitch. Work just *one* small two-CAT stitch across to the right, and then immediately skip down the back of your canvas two tracks to track W, where your needle should emerge, sharing a hole once again with your larger stitch.

Work a pair of parallel two-CAT stitches one right below the other, nestling up against and sharing holes with the parallel large dark stitches, and then skip two tracks down again. Continue down the square in this manner *(graphs 25, 26)*.

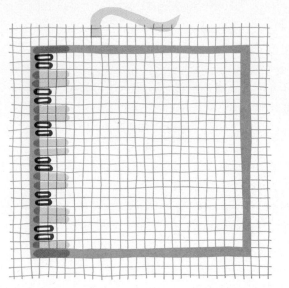

(Graph 27)

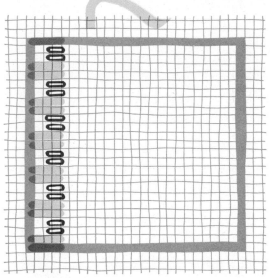

(Graph 28)

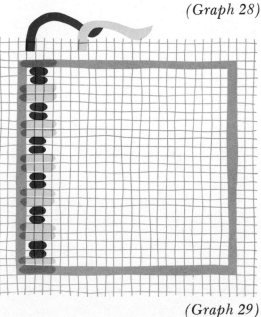

(Graph 29)

In this pattern you will find that your large stitches always nestle against the small stitches, and your dark color is against your light color. Moreover, each row should always have a *jagged edge* as you proceed across the square. One row will always protrude beyond the last *(graph 26),* until we compensate on both edges in order to get a straight line along the borders of the square on the right and on the left (NOT THIS *graph 27,* NOR THIS *graph 28,* BUT THIS *graph 29*).

57

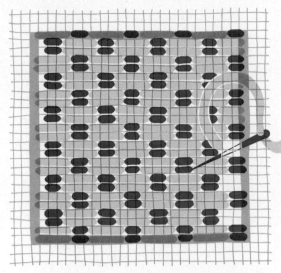

(Graph 30)

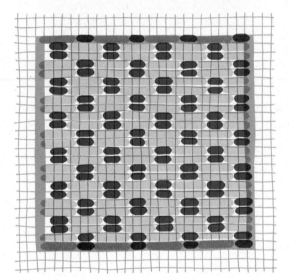

(Graph 31)

When you have gone as far as you can with the pattern, you will be stopped on the right by the pencil line, across which it is forbidden to venture. You will notice that on your left-hand side you have one canvas thread showing along the border next to each of your two-CAT stitches, and on the right side, your small stitches ended neatly on the pencil line, but you are left with three canvas threads (that is, three CATS) where you would expect to place your next row of four-CAT stitches *(graph 30)*. This calls for some compensating.

Let us start with the right side. As there is not enough room to make a four-CAT stitch with the light yarn, we have to be adaptable and make a three-CAT stitch instead to nestle against those small stitches *(graph 30)*. Use the light yarn and go up or down the final row as you would have before, always sharing a hole, never passing beyond the pencil line, and working two parallel *three*-CAT stitches which end on the pencil line on the right before skipping two tracks, and working two more parallel three-CAT stitches *(graph 31)*. Adaptability is the key word. When you come to a border that you must not pass, either because you have reached the far end of your canvas or, later, because of a design that you have in mind, just stick as closely as you can to your pattern so that you use the right color and come *as close as possible* to working the proper stitch size. In this case you should have made a four-CAT stitch if you could have, but you settled for a three-CAT stitch. You will, of course, never work a stitch *larger* than your pattern calls for.

Now let us move over to the left side where another problem faces us. Here, there is only *one* CAT uncovered, and it is right beside our first row of small dark stitches. Since the small nestle against the large, we know that in order to adhere to our pattern—and that is important—

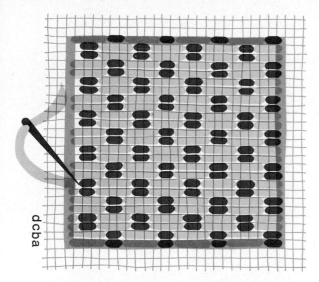

dcba

(Graph 32)

NOT THIS

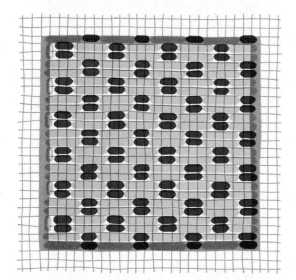

(Graph 33)

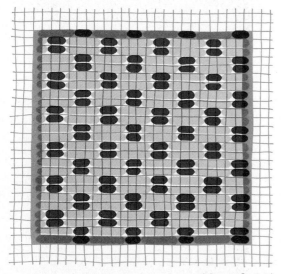

(Graph 34)

this row should be a row of light-colored large stitches. Normally they would each cover *four* CATS left to right. But this time they can only be one-CAT long, so that is how long they will be. Adaptability. Use the light yarn, come forward on track C on the left-hand pencil line, and move straight across one CAT to share a hole with that first small dark stitch. But now I am going to change the rules just a bit. Instead of emerging with your needle in the same motion when you have only *one* CAT to cover, it is better if you *do* pull your needle all the way through to the back of your canvas with *each* stitch, and keep your stitches very very loose *(graph 32)*. If you try to finish one stitch and begin the next in a single motion as before, you will find that these stitches get twisted and pinched. They are simply too small and won't look neat. This is the one case where it is best to pull the needle through to the back with each stitch. Be sure these tiny stitches are running left to right just as your other stitches did (NOT THIS *graph 33*, BUT THIS *graph 34*).

When you have completed the square, be sure that there is no yarn waiting for you. If there is, pull it through, weave it under, and snip it off. Don't be lazy about this.

Work two additional squares of the Old Florentine. This is, as you might guess from its name, a very old stitch that originated most probably in Florence, Italy. It lends itself to many color combinations. One of my students came in one day with an Old Florentine square that seemed to be a plaid. She had done all her large stitches in one color, but had alternated the rows of small stitches, using three colors, and giving a very pleasing effect. Another student came in and told me that her daughter had pointed out to her that there was a "flower" hidden in her first square of Old Florentine. "Can't you see it?" she had asked. Her mother did see it, and

worked her square in such a way that the flower blossomed forth. You may see other things in this square. Try different combinations of color; you may surprise even yourself at what lovely effects emerge. It is experimentation that makes every sampler unique.

How, why and where to use the Old Florentine Stitch

The Old Florentine pattern, like the Brick Stitch pattern, can be enlarged to a six-CAT stitch and a three-CAT stitch or miniaturized to a two-CAT stitch and a one-CAT stitch, and it moves along quite quickly. Used in one color, it is a bit busier than the Brick Stitch, and therefore is not quite as neutral a background stitch, but it can be used as such where the central design tends to be simple and bold, not overly complex. Its ease of compensating is helpful when used as a background stitch, but it might become a bit competitive if it is used to surround a very detailed or delicate central design.

On the other hand, precisely because this stitch is a bit more complex than the Brick Stitch, it needs less color and planning to stand on its own. Simply by adding some interesting colors, it can be used to cover the entire surface of a relatively small decorative item, such as an eye-glass case or jewelry case. The Brick Stitch pattern is so flexible that you can do almost anything with it. The Old Florentine, on the other hand, does not easily lend itself to the formation of complex designs. If you can use its two large parallel stitches followed by two small parallel stitches to form a design with color, it is an appropriate stitch. But if you like to plan and

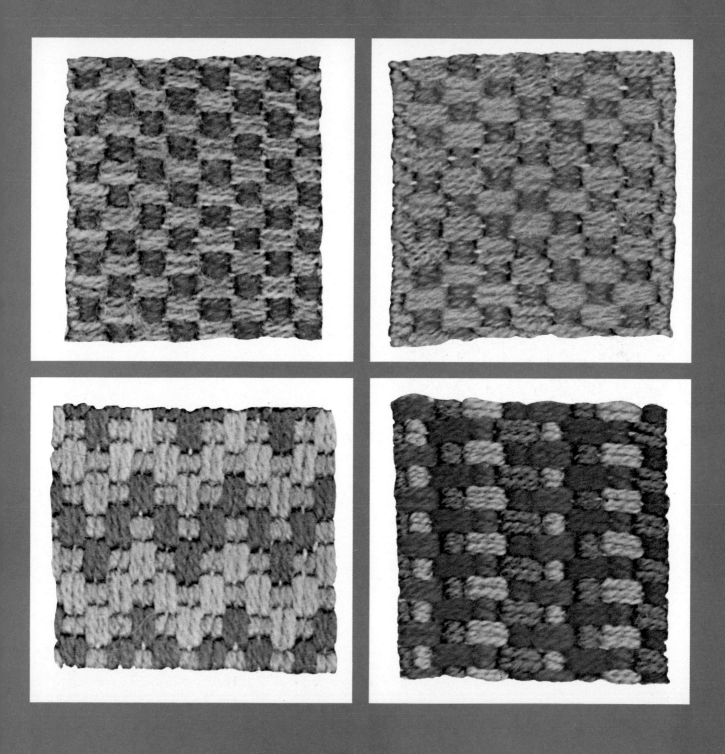

count and work out complicated designs, the Old Florentine may prove to be too difficult.

It is a tighter stitch than the Brick because of the two-CAT stitches, but the larger stitches might snag if used on an item that gets a lot of wear and tear. For a purse or eyeglass case, for instance, it would be best either to miniaturize the stitch or do it on a smaller canvas, perhaps a 16- or 18-mesh to the inch, so the stitches would be smaller.

The Old Florentine pattern is quite fast moving, requiring only about one-third the number of stitches that would be used if you were to fill in a given area with the basic needlepoint stitch (BNS).

In short, the Old Florentine Stitch seems to be saying to us: "I like myself pretty much the way I am. Do not try to change me too much, for I will work best for you in the shape I am presently in."

For some lovely examples of the Old Florentine, see pages 47, 127.

The Parisian Stitch

How to do the Parisian Stitch

Sometimes students are confused by the idea of counting "CATS," or canvas threads, instead of holes. Counting holes is impossible, as you will learn with more experience in different forms of stitchery. One student was having such a difficult time counting four CATS that I stood behind her as she worked and said, "Let me help you. I will touch each CAT with the needle as you count to four. All right?" She nodded miserably and as I touched each CAT in turn, she began, "One, three, two. . . ."

Talk about being confused! But that woman is now doing beautiful work, and although she will remain forever anonymous, her work is displayed prominently in this book. So take heart ye of small faith or faltering count.

The Old Florentine, which you have just completed, has been called the double Parisian, and you will soon see why. The two stitches are quite similar, although the finished look is completely different.

We shall try using three colors at this time: dark, medium, and light. I use these designations to make clear which row we are working on, but the reader may, of course, decide to use three

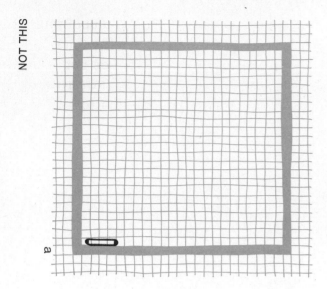

(Graph 1)

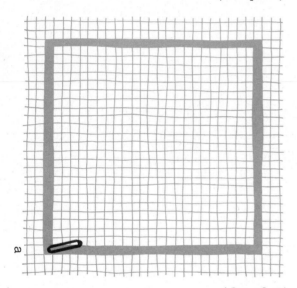

(Graph 2)

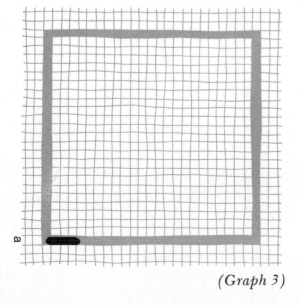

(Graph 3)

colors of similar intensity, for example, soft pink, soft turquoise, and white. Whatever your colors, be consistent in following directions. In this chapter we have used purple for dark, blue for medium, and pink for light.

In teaching each square I am primarily concerned with teaching the reader a *pattern* of stitches, not the maximum use of color and design. That part comes later and is left to the imagination of the learner. Once you have the pattern of the stitch firmly in mind, there are an infinite number of possible variations and adaptations that can be made. The accompanying photographs just skim the surface of possibilities.

Thread up with your dark yarn (three ply of Persian) and bring your needle to the front of your canvas in the lower left-hand corner where the left and bottom pencil lines meet.

Bring your needle straight across track A, covering four CATS and being careful not to slant your stitch (NOT THIS *graph 1,* NOR THIS *graph 2,* BUT THIS *graph 3*).

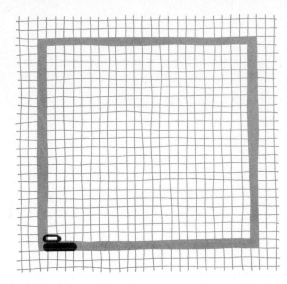

(Graph 4)

Insert your needle and emerge on the front of your canvas, again in the same motion, on the track directly above—track B—but this time do not come up on the left-hand pencil line (NOT THIS *graph 4,* BUT THIS *graph 5*), but one CAT to the right of it *(graph 6).*

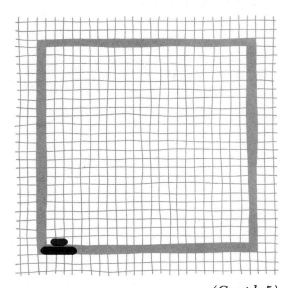

(Graph 5)

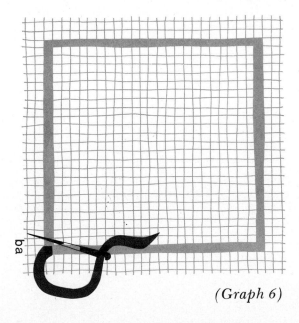

(Graph 6)

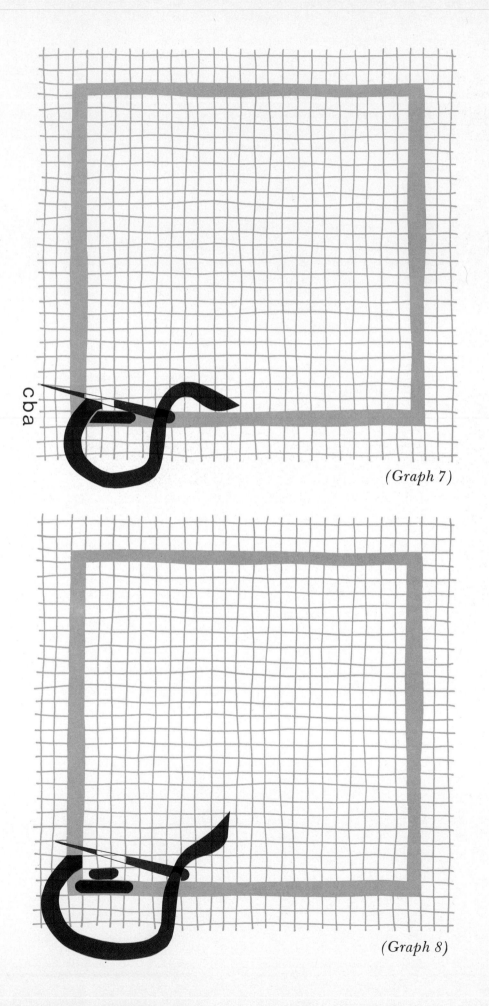

cba

(Graph 7)

(Graph 8)

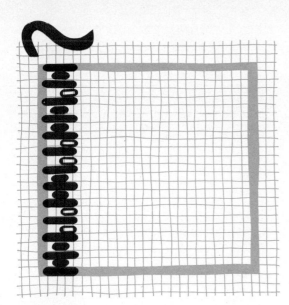

Work your stitch straight across two CATS on track B, insert and emerge on track C *right on the pencil line (graph 7).*

Work a four-CAT stitch and bring your needle to the front of the canvas one CAT in from the pencil line, ready to make another two-CAT stitch *(graph 8).*

(Graph 9)

As you work you will being to see the pattern emerge: a large four-CAT stitch, then just above it and set midway over it, a small two-CAT stitch, then a large, then a small, and so on. The smaller stitch is one CAT shorter, at both the beginning and the end of the larger stitch. Stated differently, the four-CAT stitch extends beyond the two-CAT stitch at either end; therefore, there should always be a jagged edge as your work proceeds, never a straight edge (NOT THIS *graph 9,* BUT THIS *graph 10).*

(Graph 10)

Continue this pattern all the way up to the top of your square. Your last stitch, directly *on* the top pencil line, will be a large four-CAT stitch (*graphs 11, 12, 13*).

If you have enough yarn in your needle to use again, bring your needle through to the front of the canvas in a free spot nearby, allowing the leftover yarn to wait until you need your dark color again.

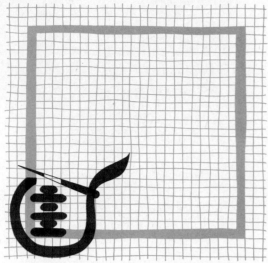

(Graph 11)

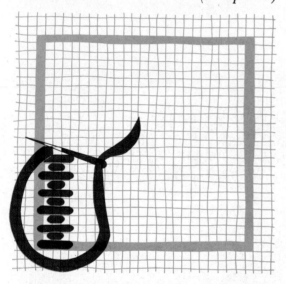

(Graph 12)

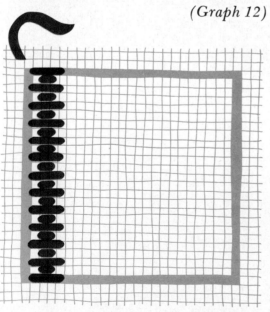

(Graph 13)

The background of this tennis racket cover is BNS while the lamb is worked in Parisian Stitch to achieve a fluffy texture.

Ontario's official flower is the Trillium. This handsome example is worked in BNS with Brick background.

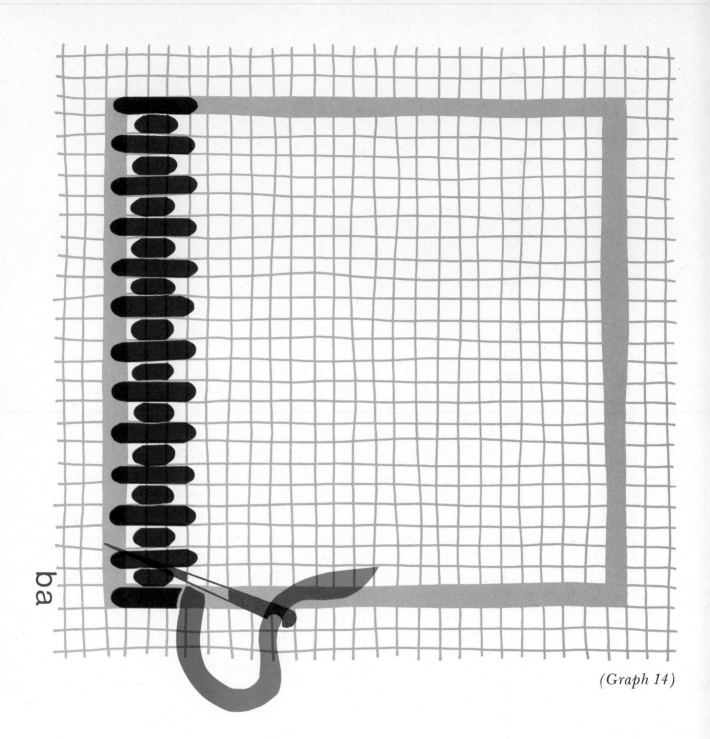

ba

(Graph 14)

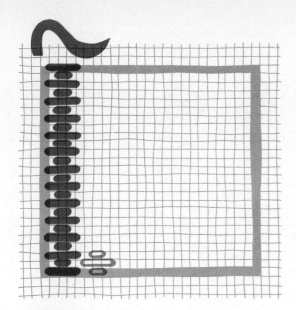

(Graph 15)

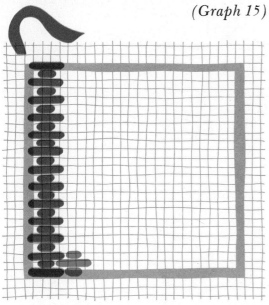

(Graph 16)

Now, thread up with your medium color. Start the first stitch of the second row by pulling your needle through to the front on the bottom pencil line—track A—sharing a hole with your first dark four-CAT stitch, but this time begin with a two-CAT stitch and emerge again on track B, sharing a hole *(graph 14),* and ready to work a four-CAT stitch. Be sure to share holes or you will have canvas showing (NOT THIS *graph 15,* BUT THIS *graph 16*).

Continue up the canvas, working a two-CAT medium-color stitch, then a four-CAT, then a two-CAT, right up to and including your top pencil line *(graphs 17, 18, 19)*.

Remember, when you are running out of a strand of yarn, don't be frugal. Change to a new strand before your leftover piece gets too small and your final stitches look pinched and twisted.

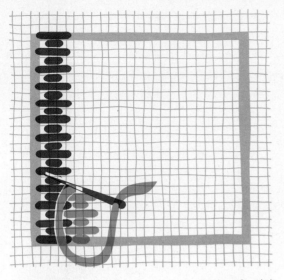

(Graph 17)

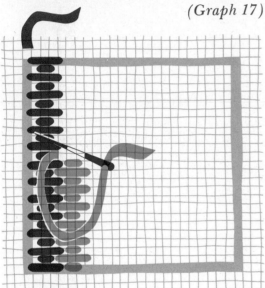

(Graph 18)

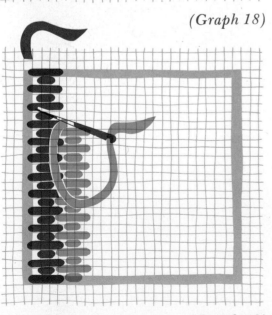

(Graph 19)

NOT THIS

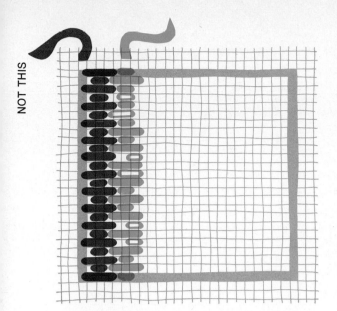

(Graph 20)

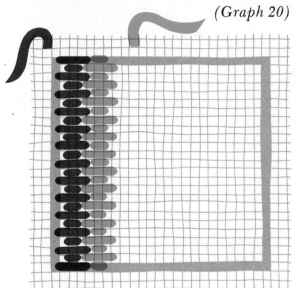

(Graph 21)

Notice that in the Parisian pattern your larger stitches nestle beside your small stitches and vice versa. And once again, you always have a jagged line at the far edges (NOT THIS *graph 20*, BUT THIS *graph 21*).

Be sure that the tension of your stitches is as even as you can make it. Your stitches should not be loose, loopy, or lumpy—the three bad L's. Nor should they be taut, tight, and twisted—the evil T's that pull the canvas out of shape. It was surprising to discover that the newcomer to needlepoint is more likely to make his or her stitches too loose, rather than too tight, but this does not mean that I do not come across the occasional student who gives such a strong yank with each stitch that one can almost hear the canvas groan in pain as it twists out of shape. Don't be too hard on the canvas, but don't be too restrained either. Pull on the strand until you feel a gentle pressure from the canvas. The yarn should lie close to the canvas threads, but not distort them.

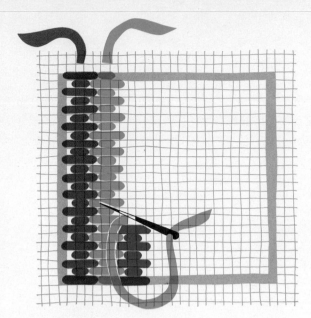

(Graph 22)

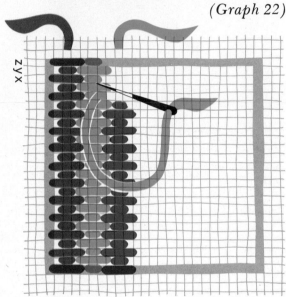

(Graph 23)

When you have completed your second row, pull your remaining yarn forward to wait for you, and thread up with your lightest yarn. This time you begin on the bottom pencil line with a four-CAT stitch, then a two-CAT stitch immediately above, then a four-CAT stitch again, and in this same manner proceed up the canvas, always being sure that you are sharing holes with the stitches of the previous row *(graphs 22, 23)*. You will notice that your square is beginning to reveal a lovely pattern of interlocking stripes. Later on you may want to count the number of stripes in the square and build a color scheme around them, but for now let's stay with three colors and finish the square.

The fourth row will be done in the dark color. Pull the strand that is waiting for you at the top of the square through to the back and thread up. Weave it under across the back so that there will not be a large loop where you have brought it over, and start the same pattern, but work it from top to bottom this time.

Bring your needle through to the front on the top pencil line and share a hole with your last light-colored stitch. As you may have judged from the emerging pattern, you start with a two-CAT stitch straight across, then a four-CAT stitch on the track just below and so on, down to and including the bottom pencil line.

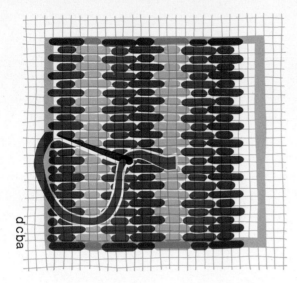

d c b a

(Graph 24)

When you have completed as many full rows as you can, you must survey the jagged edges on either side and decide which color will conform to the pattern you have set. In our pattern of dark, medium, light, dark, medium, light, we find that light always comes before dark, and medium always comes after dark *(graph 24)*. Therefore, to compensate on the left-hand side, use the light color.

As with the compensation for the Old Florentine pattern, you cover one CAT only, so do remember to pull your yarn through to the back with each stitch, instead of emerging to the front again in one motion. As I mentioned in the previous chapter but will state again because repetition is the core of learning, pulling the yarn through to the back with each stitch is an exception to the rule; otherwise your stitches will look tight and twisted. In fact, when covering one CAT only, it is necessary to hold your canvas up and let your needle and yarn dangle frequently in order to keep your yarn from twisting. And you must keep those tiny stitches looser than you think or they will still look too tight. The only other exception to the rule, by the way, is when you are working needlepoint on a frame, and then you generally have to pull your needle all the way through to the back because the canvas is held so stiffly. This is why I don't recommend using a frame unless you are working on a very large and heavy piece that cannot be carried about.

To compensate that left-hand side, start on row B at the pencil line and move to your right across one CAT, sharing a hole with your first small dark stitch.

After you have pulled your yarn through to the back loosely, come forward again two tracks up—track D—and work another one-CAT stitch and so on all the way up *(graph 24)*.

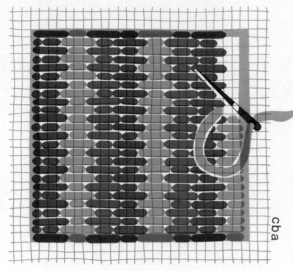

(Graph 25)

Weave your light yarn under the back and snip it off close to the canvas. You will not be needing it again for this square.

Now to compensate on the right side. Since the row just before was a dark color, thread up with the medium color. If you have some waiting for you, pull it through to the back and use it. Starting at track A on the bottom, share a hole with the large dark stitch. In the Parisian pattern this stitch should be a two-CAT stitch, so work a two-CAT stitch and come up, sharing a hole on your next row.

Now we cannot do a four-CAT stitch because the pencil line interferes at three CATS. Therefore, we must adapt ourselves to this new situation and cover the three CATS. On this compensating row you will work a two-CAT stitch and then a three-CAT stitch all the way up to the final top (or bottom) track *(graph 25)*.

When the square is completed, weave your yarn ends in and snip off. There should not be any yarn hanging out from the front of the canvas, like so many horse's tails. When you no longer need your leftover strands, pull them through to the back, one by one, weave them under, and snip them off.

Your sampler should now have two completed squares of Brick Stitch, three of Old Florentine, and one of Parisian. Work two more Parisian squares; the design possibilities are endless, once you have the pattern clearly set in your mind. Every little diamond motif might vary in color to form a potpourri of color, or use repetitions of the same color to achieve a special effect. That is up to you. See how adventuresome you can be, but never lose sight of the essential pattern. If you remember that the Parisian tends to form stripes, it may help you in planning your colors.

One more warning: Don't jump from chapter to chapter, learning new stitches one right after the other, without doing these extra two or three squares. If you do, you will lose the pattern formed in your mind, and you will only recall a jumble of stitches. It is important to hold back and practice each stitch in the extra squares before continuing on to the next stitch pattern. In this way, you will not only learn the various patterns, you will *remember* them, which is more important. It is also very important that you feel confident enough with the special rhythm of each pattern to experiment with design and color, and this can only be achieved with practice. In fact, you may soon find yourself lying awake at night and mentally working out ideas for these squares. The next morning, if you are not too exhausted, you may find graph paper helpful in working out a complicated design.

How, why and where to use the Parisian Stitch

The Parisian Stitch pattern is quite versatile, being decorative and at the same time fast moving and easy to compensate. As a one-color background for a simple motif, it has a lovely textured effect that does not detract from a bold, straightforward central design. Its pleasant texture will set the basic needlepoint stitch (BNS) into relief, so the two combine very well.

On the other hand, the multicolored Parisian Stitch is decorative enough to stand on its own anywhere that stripes are indicated—for a belt, luggage rack straps, or as a border for almost any decorative item.

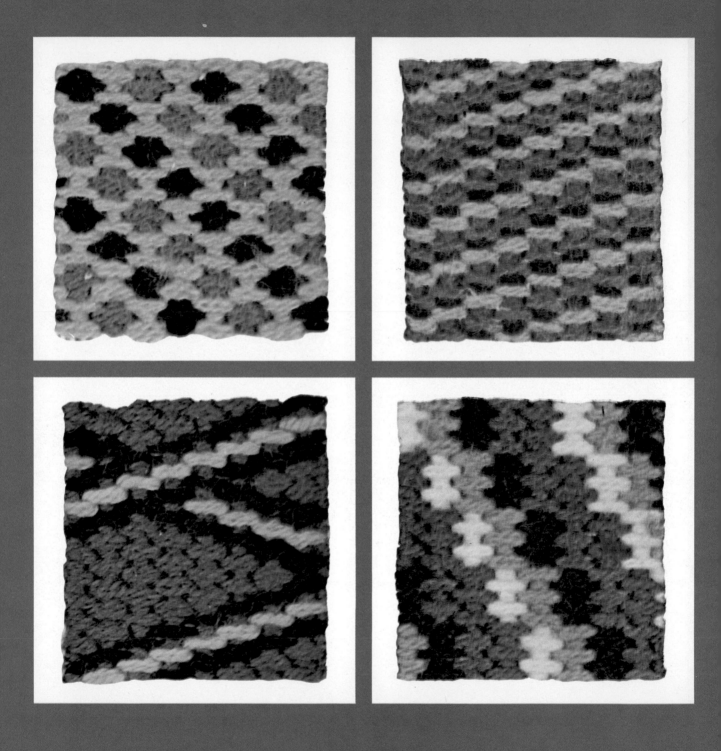

The Parisian Stitch is a good deal tighter than the Brick Stitch and somewhat tighter than the Old Florentine and will take more use and abuse. I would not use it on 10- or 12-mesh for a rug, but on 14- or 16-mesh it would be fine. Similarly, an eyeglass case that gets a lot of handling would best be done on 14-mesh, but a pillow with a Parisian background is fine on 10- or 12-mesh canvas.

Relative to the basic needlepoint stitch (BNS), the Parisian works up 65 percent faster, quite a saving in time and effort, and if your canvas design can benefit from this stitch, it is delightfully easy to use.

Compensating, as we have seen, is not difficult. If you are using the Parisian as a background stitch, the pattern may seem formless around the central motif. But this is of no consequence as the eye of the observer tends to pick up the outer pattern and continue it in the mind's eye.

In sum, the Parisian is best used in one color as a background stitch, where it provides lovely texture and movement, or standing on its own, carefully planned as to color and design. It is not a marvelously decorative stitch in and of itself; color and planning are needed to bring out its many beautiful possibilities.

To find examples of this lovely stitch, see pages 71, 127, 173, 213, 214.

LESSON
4

The
Hungarian
Point
Stitch

How to do the Hungarian Point Stitch

This stitch closely resembles the Parisian—but with a difference! We will do it in two colors, a dark and a medium, of full three-ply Persian. In this chapter we use blue for the dark and pink for the medium.

The first stitch is a small two-CAT stitch that begins on the bottom pencil line *but* one CAT in from the lower left-hand pencil line. That is, this stitch does *not* begin in your exact corner as all the others have (NOT THIS *graph 1,* BUT THIS *graph 2).*

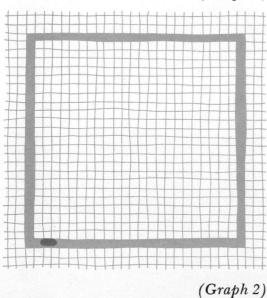

(Graph 1)

(Graph 2)

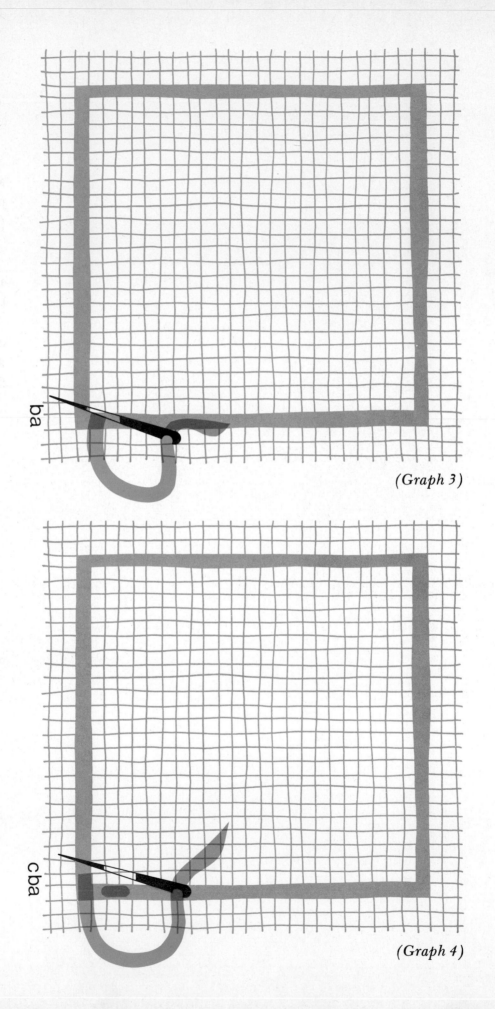

ba

(Graph 3)

cba

(Graph 4)

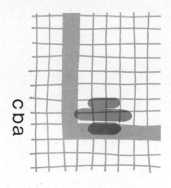

cba

(Graph 5)

Thread up with your dark yarn and bring your needle through from the back of the canvas to the front, one CAT in from the left-hand pencil line and *on* the bottom pencil line.

Insert your needle across two CATS to your right and come up again forward of the canvas, in one motion, right *on* the left-hand pencil line this time, on the very next track—track B *(graph 3)*.

Work a four-CAT stitch straight across track B, insert your needle, and emerge on track C, one CAT *in* from the pencil line *(graph 4)*.

Work another small two-CAT stitch. As with the Parisian, the two-CAT stitch sits midway across and on top of the larger four-CAT stitch just below *(graph 5)*.

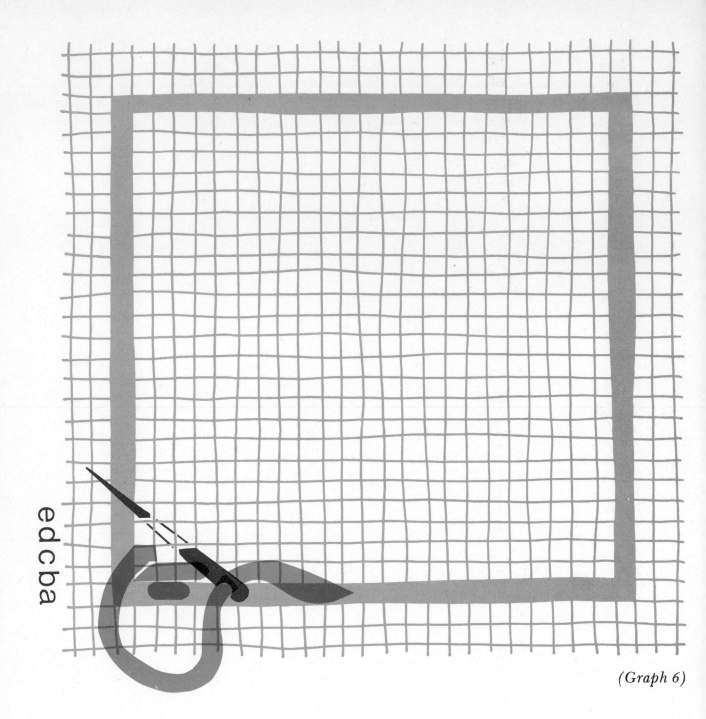

edcba

(Graph 6)

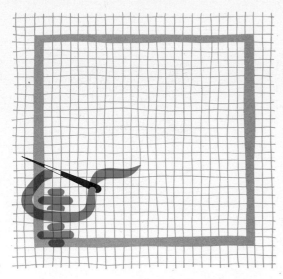

(Graph 7)

But here's where we differ from the Parisian. As you complete your little diamond motif of small stitch, large stitch, small stitch, angle your needle across the back of your canvas, *skip a track,* and emerge one CAT in from the left pencil line on track E *(graph 6).*

Repeat the motif: work a two-CAT stitch, emerge on the pencil line, and work a four-CAT stitch, emerge one CAT in from the pencil line and work a two-CAT stitch, and then once again skip a track. Emerge one CAT in from the pencil line, prepared to start your next diamond motif with a two-CAT stitch *(graph 7).*

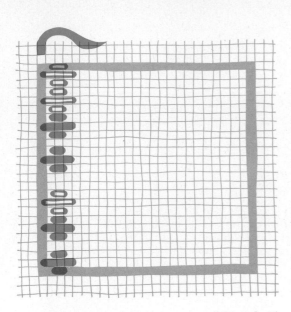

Don't forget to skip that row after completing each motif (NOT THIS *graph 8*), and be sure that your larger stitches extend beyond your little stitches at both ends (NOR THIS *graph 9,* BUT THIS *graph 10*).

(Graph 8)

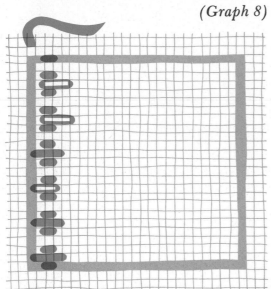

(Graph 9)

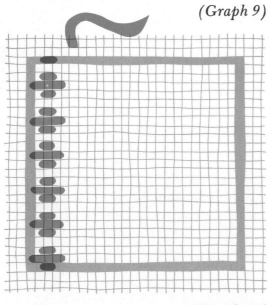

(Graph 10)

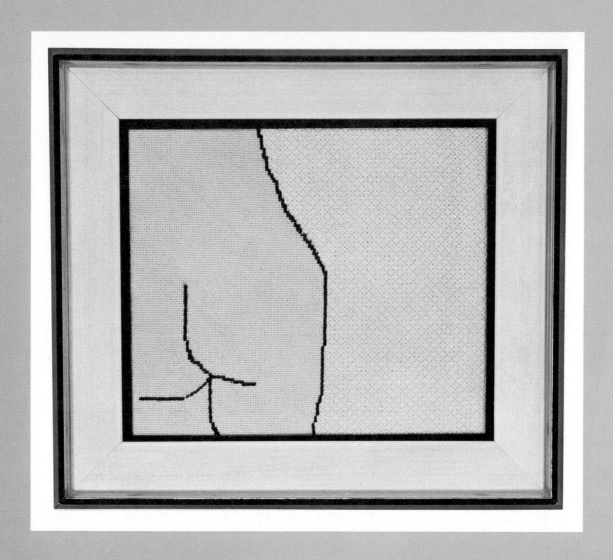

A nude, after Picasso, with a white background worked in Hungarian Point achieves a stunning effect.

Here the sampler surrounds a BNS center. The doll's face—
on the Queen Anne chair covered in a Bargello design—and tote
are worked in BNS. Pigpen (of cartoon fame) and the blue
carnation pillow are done in Brick background, while the
Mosaic-background butterfly pillow has a frame of Oblong
Cross with Backstitch. "Diana" is bordered in Hungarian
Ground. See plate on page 229 for brick cover detail.

(Graph 11)

(Graph 12)

Continue this pattern right up to and including the top pencil line *(graphs 11, 12)*.

You will notice that in doing this 2–4–2–skip pattern you are simply expanding and contracting your stitches at both ends by one CAT and then skipping a row and repeating the process. Once you realize this, it may be easier for you to picture the stitch so that you don't have to count once you get started, but can simply reach one CAT outward or inward on either side of your stitch as you go along. But people learn differently and conceptualize differently, and where this concept may make it much easier for one person, it may be meaningless to another. The important thing is to learn the stitch. This is all that matters, and if you have done this, it doesn't matter a hoot if you can describe it or not.

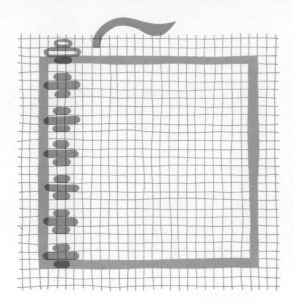

(Graph 13)

If you have done it correctly, you will end with one small two-CAT stitch, the start of a new diamond motif that could not be finished because your border interfered (NOT THIS *graph 13*). Refer to *graph 15* to see how your first row should look.

Pull your leftover yarn through to the front to wait for you and thread up with your medium-colored yarn.

The beginning of this second row may puzzle you a bit, but it is dictated by the size of the square, which isn't large enough to allow for only completed diamond motifs. Just as we had to end our first row with a single two-CAT stitch, so we have to begin our second row with a single two-CAT stitch as if it were the final stitch of a previous motif.

Bring your needle through to the front of the canvas, on the bottom pencil line, and share a hole with your first small dark stitch *(graph 14)*.

Insert your needle across two CATs to the right, and *immediately* skip a track, to track C, share a hole with your second small dark stitch *(graph 15)*.

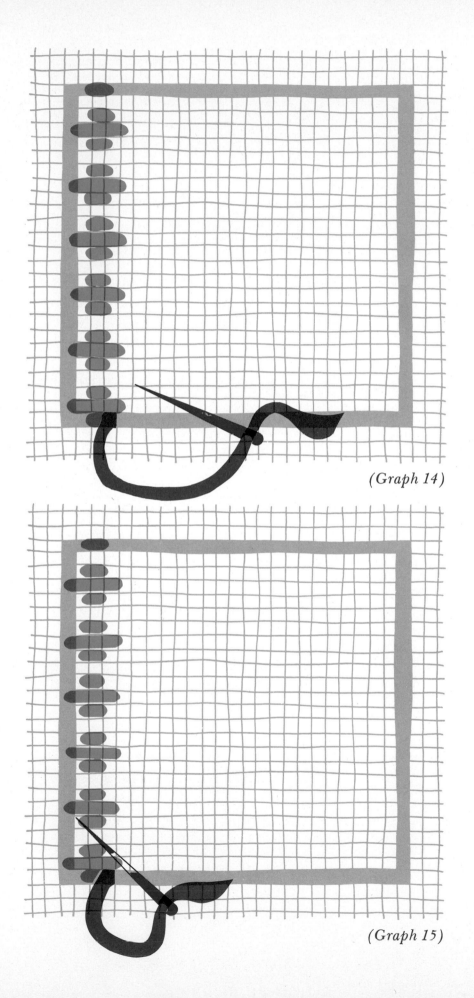

(Graph 14)

(Graph 15)

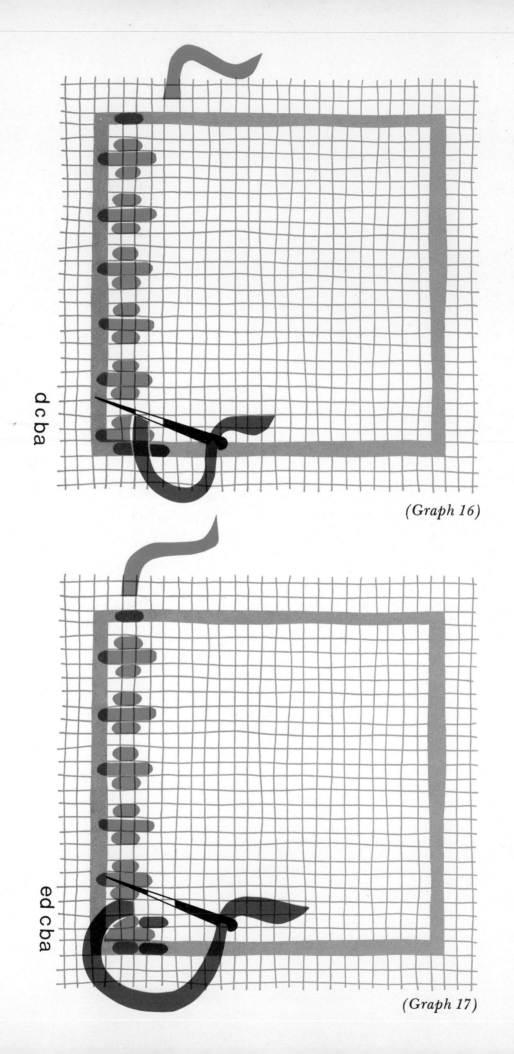

d c b a

(Graph 16)

ed cba

(Graph 17)

96

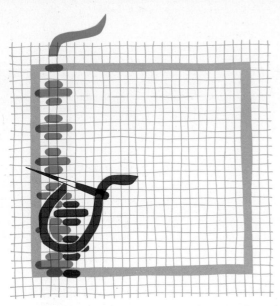

(Graph 18)

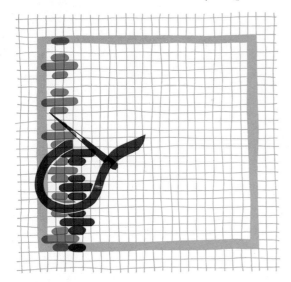

(Graph 19)

Begin the complete motif. Work a small two-CAT stitch, emerge on the next track—track **D**—which has no stitches in it as yet *(graph 16)*, expand your just finished small stitch by one CAT on either end so that you come to the front of your canvas two CATS in from the pencil line, work a four-CAT stitch, and in one motion emerge again to share a hole on track E *(graph 17)*.

Now complete your motif with a two-CAT stitch. At this point you must skip a track and start again with a two-CAT stitch that shares a hole, expand that stitch into the former empty track to begin your four-CAT stitch *(graph 18)*, and then on the next track, share a hole for your small stitch before skipping a track once again *(graph 19)*.

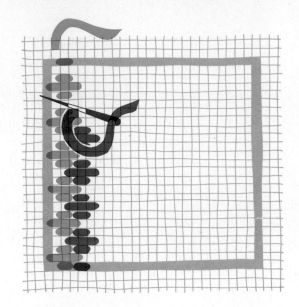

(Graph 20)

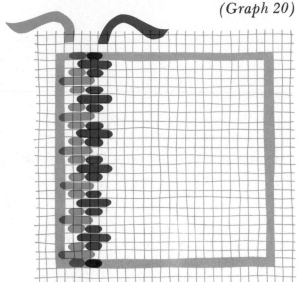

(Graph 21)

Work your way up the canvas in this manner until you reach the top of the square *(graphs 20, 21)*.

Thread up with your dark yarn for the third row. If you are starting from the top with leftover yarn, share a hole with your last medium-color stitch, and on your way down the row, just follow the configuration of your previous dark-yarn row. As it ended with one small stitch at the top, you must begin with one small stitch. Then, as it skips a row, you must do so too and begin your diamond motif on track X with a two-CAT–four-CAT–two-CAT pattern, always sharing holes, of course. Then skip a row and repeat the magic numbers all the way down to the bottom *(graphs 22, 23)*. If you run out of yarn, you should know what to do by now: Pull your end through, weave it under the back, and snip it off close to the canvas.

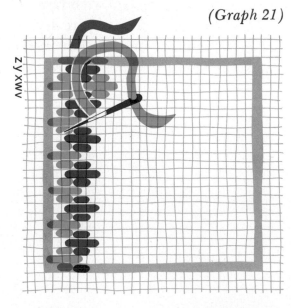

(Graph 22)

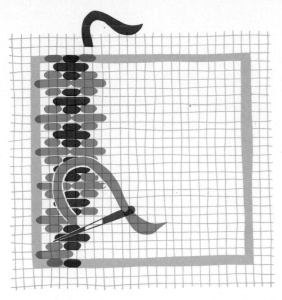

(Graph 23)

For your fourth row, if you have medium-color yarn waiting for you, pull it through to the back, thread up, and once again do what you did on the previous medium-color yarn row. In other words, every even-numbered row looks like every other previous even-numbered row, and every odd-numbered row looks like its fellow odd-numbered rows. At the top of your previous medium-colored row, you ended with a complete diamond motif, did you not? (I hope you did!) Therefore, now you will start right on the top pencil line, sharing a hole, and commence your 2–4–2–skip pattern all the way down the square (graphs 24, 25).

Like the Parisian, you should always have a jagged edge on the left that you will have to compensate when you have finished working the body of the square.

Now that you are becoming quite experienced, perhaps you can figure out how to compensate this square. If so, go to it. But if you feel a bit unsure, follow these directions.

On the left-hand side you will use medium-color yarn. Thread up, and let's begin at the bottom. As with most of these squares, you can begin either at the top or bottom, but as you have no yarn waiting for you at the left of your square, let's start at the bottom. Emerge exactly in the lower left-hand corner where the two pencil lines meet.

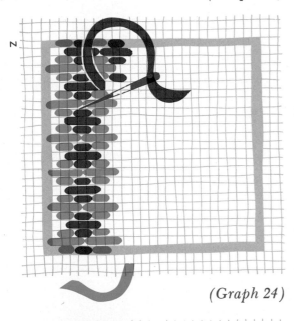

(Graph 24)

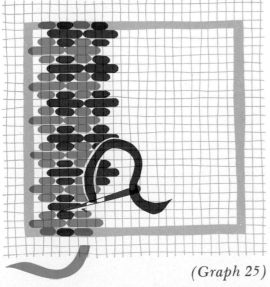

(Graph 25)

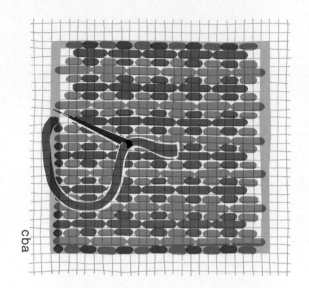

cba

(Graph 26)

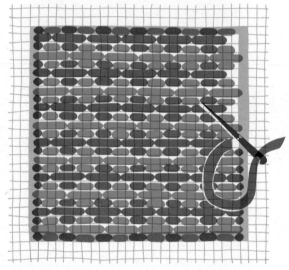

(Graph 27)

Work a one-CAT stitch across to the right, pulling your thread through to the back very loosely, which, as you know is necessary when covering a single CAT. Emerge then on track C, skipping a track, and as you cannot work a full diamond motif, you will work what you can, which is essentially a half diamond motif of one CAT–two CATS–one CAT.

Skip a row and repeat this pattern *(graph 26)*. Work this abbreviated motif as far as you can, then pull your yarn through to the back, weave it under, and snip it off.

On the right side, with medium-color yarn, use your leftover yarn if you have a strand waiting for you, and cover whatever canvas is showing. Here, if you start at the bottom, you will do what you did on the left. Start by covering one CAT, pull your yarn loosely through to the back, and then emerge two tracks up to begin your abbreviated diamond motif pattern of one CAT–two CATS–one CAT–skip, and repeat it all the way up to the top *(graph 27)*.

Now you have finished one square in Hungarian Point. Although it worked quite similarly to the Parisian, it has a different feel, doesn't it? It forms a pattern of closely locked diamonds instead of stripes. In clear colors it often seems to me to have a medieval armorial look about it.

Work two more squares in the Hungarian Point. You should consider now the placement of your squares and the color balance. Try not to use too much of any one color on one side of your sampler.

Do give your canvas a quarter turn every now and again before commencing a new square so that your stitches will not all seem to move in the same direction. At this point, it does not matter where the top or the bottom of your canvas will be. But it is nonetheless important to keep color and pattern as balanced as possible. But balance, as I mentioned before, does not imply perfect symmetry. Your sampler can have lots of variety and still achieve balance.

How, why and where to use the Hungarian Point Stitch

The Hungarian Point is an enormously decorative stitch when worked in a riot of colors. It can stand beautifully on its own for an eyeglass case, jewelry case, or tennis racket cover. Worked several inches deep, it would make a lovely border for a rug or a pillow. It is quite a tight stitch, and used on 14-mesh canvas, it would take a great deal of wear. It works about 60 percent faster than the basic needlepoint stitch (BNS); it works up so quickly in fact that eyeglass cases can be made in a day or two, and they make a wonderfully decorative gift. An initial might be placed in a square worked in the basic needlepoint stitch (BNS) on one side of your case, and the rest might be worked in Hungarian Point.

Worked in a solid color, the pattern is sufficiently set and textured to make an interesting background stitch around a central motif that is not overly complex. It can be used in concert with other decorative stitches to form a pillow or tapestry of great beauty. Done in browns and rusts, it takes on an earthy Indian feeling. Done in a regular color sequence, it begins to run in diagonal rows, as you can see from some of the photographs. If you have

a mathematical sense, you can make this stitch work for you in any way that you please to form all sorts of fascinating geometric designs.

The Hungarian Point may be a bit more difficult to compensate than the others, but if your central motif is not too irregular, it should not prove too much of an obstacle.

In sum, the Hungarian Point pattern, though suitable as a neutral background stitch for a bold forthright design, is also able to stand on its own. It does not demand much planning of design because its own decorative nature will make this pattern stand out by the use of color alone.

Study pages 47, 91, 113, 115, 127, and 214 to see creative usage of the Hungarian Point.

LESSON
5

The Encroaching Upright Gobelin Stitch

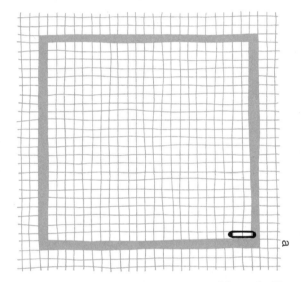

(Graph 1)

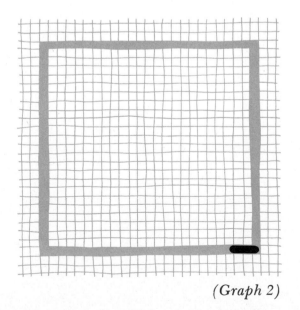

(Graph 2)

How to do the Encroaching Upright Gobelin Stitch

The Encroaching Upright Gobelin stitch is most effective when worked in a range of shades of one color. For example if you are using three blues, start with the darkest, or if you are using five golds, start with the darkest. Thread up in *two* ply only. This stitch is a special relaxation after your efforts with the Hungarian Point. It is quite simple, although very different from the others.

In this chapter we will use three shades from dark to light; purple, blue, and pink, in that order.

Select any available square. We are going to begin this stitch in the lower *right*-hand corner for a change of pace. Count three CATS in from the lower *right*-hand corner and emerge on the bottom pencil line. It is quite necessary that you learn how to count those CATS. If you count, "one, three, two," as my pupil did, you are sure to come through in the wrong spot, so count carefully. Are you right ON the bottom pencil (NOT THIS *graph 1,* BUT THIS *graph 2*)? Are you three CATS in from the corner?

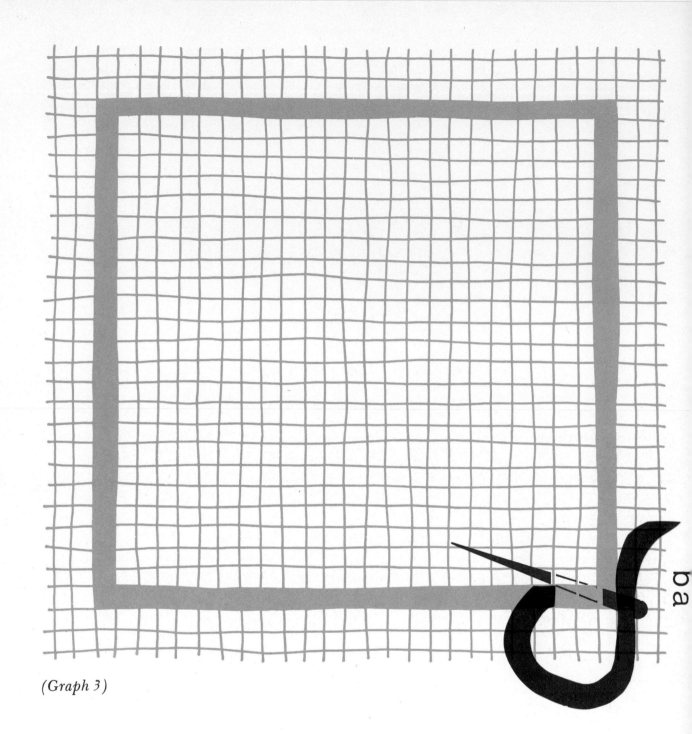

(Graph 3)

ba

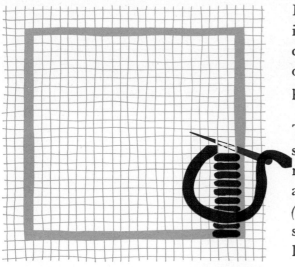

Bring your yarn straight across the three CATS and insert your needle directly in the right-hand corner, emerging again just above your first stitch on track B, once again three CATS in from the pencil line *(graph 3)*.

This first row of the Gobelin Encroaching is very simple, as you just continue to work one stitch right above the last, each stitch covering three CATS and reaching to the right-hand pencil line *(graph 4)*. Move right on up your canvas, being sure to cover the top pencil line before pulling the leftover yarn forward to wait for you *(graph 5)*.

(Graph 4)

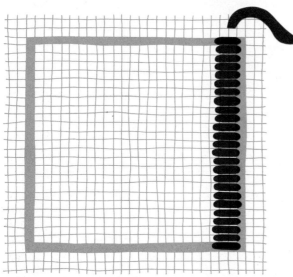

(Graph 5)

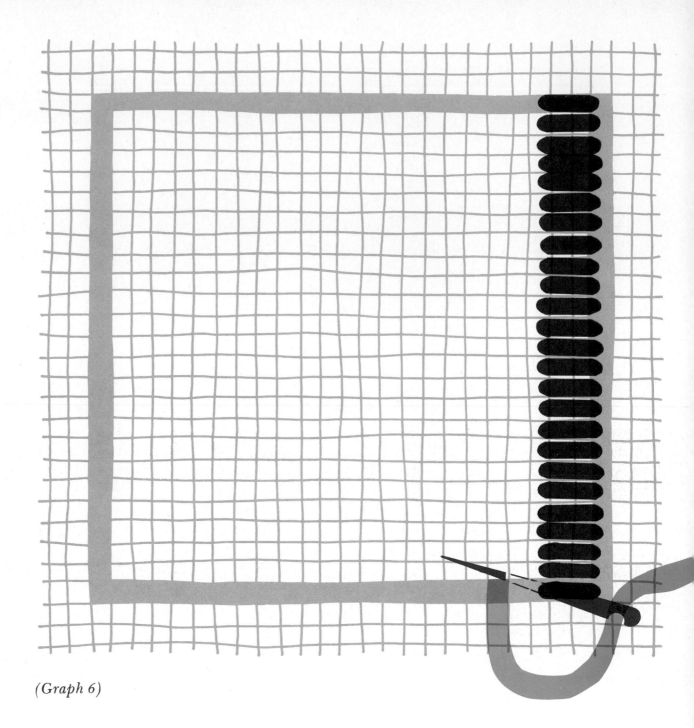

(Graph 6)

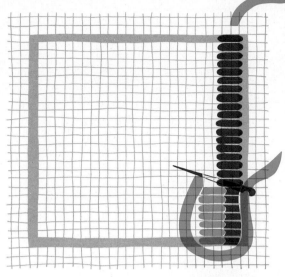

(Graph 7)

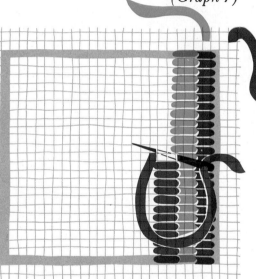

(Graph 8)

With two ply again, thread up with your next color, which should be slightly lighter than the first. Start your second row on the bottom pencil line again, but this time emerge only TWO CATS to the left of the completed stitch. Bring your needle through to the front of your canvas, but instead of sharing a hole as you did with the other stitches, go past the shared hole, moving a total of three CATS to the right *(graph 6)*. This means that you actually encroach, or go right over and on top of, your previous stitch, inserting your needle *through* the previous stitch. In doing this, do not push the previous stitch aside to find the hole, but rather feel for the proper hole with your needle, and then splice right through the thread of the first stitch. We use two ply for this stitch because we can split it quite evenly and easily.

You will probably find your own method for locating the hidden hole. Some people count each CAT. This is not easy because two of the CATS are obvious, but the other CAT is hidden beneath the stitches of the first row. Other people have a good enough eye to gauge the size of each stitch once they have correctly counted the first two stitches. I run my needle ever so lightly into the "shared" hole and then slide it into the next hole to the right.

After inserting your needle into and splitting the first stitch on the bottom pencil line, work right on up the row, emerging one track at a time, TWO CATS to the left of the completed stitch, and moving three CATS to the right, encroaching upon the previous stitch *(graph 7)*.

Your third row is the same as the second. Begin with your next lightest shade, emerge two CATS to the left of the completed stitch on the bottom pencil line, and move up your square, working the same stitch on every track right up to the top *(graph 8)*.

111

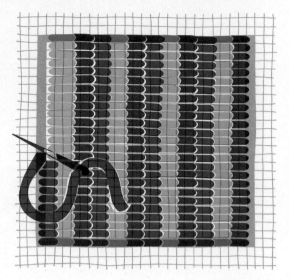

(Graph 9)

Continue in this pattern until your square is completed. When you have worked your lightest yarn, go back to your darkest again. If a leftover strand is waiting for you at the top, pull it through to the back, thread up, and weave it under a few stitches toward where you intend to emerge so as not to leave a big loop on the back. Then come through to the front of your canvas, two CATS to the left of your top stitch, and work the Encroaching Stitch down the canvas.

As this stitch does not have a jagged edge, you should not have any problem with compensating. When you reach your final row, you will find that you have only one CAT exposed. This is as it should be.

Emerge on the left-hand pencil line and work a TWO-CAT stitch, encroaching all the way up the row, just as you did with your three-CAT stitch *(graph 9)*. It will look right when you are finished because only two CATS of each stitch ever remain exposed after you have encroached, and that is what will show on this final row.

This stitch is lovely for delicately running one color into another. Work two additional squares in the Encroaching Gobelin, and experiment a bit with different ways of using color tones.

How, why and where to use the Encroaching Upright Gobelin Stitch

The Encroaching Gobelin is one of the oldest stitches. It was used exclusively on many ancient tapestries because it is an exceptionally tight stitch, with each row tying down the one before, and because it gives a lovely range of shading, a very important element in early tapestries. Some of my pupils love its flat, shaded look; others find it dull

Here the Encroaching Stitch forms the doll's hair. Her apron is Hungarian Ground—dress of Mosaic with scattered red Cross Stitches. The butterfly belt is Brick backgrounded and the pillow uses Mini-Brick, Parisian, and Mosaic.

and lacking in texture. However you feel about it, it is a useful stitch to know, and it can be worked slanted as well as straight for a slightly different effect.

Imagine, for example, a jungle scene with a background of about twenty rows of a midnight blue shading into sixteen rows of a royal dark blue, twelve rows of a medium blue, eight rows of light blue shading into pale blue, and then perhaps five rows of pale pink shading into a few rows of a deeper pink, and so on, to simulate a sunset. The colors can be as varied as you choose to make them

Color combination is important to all stitches, but it is vital to this one. We have often noted in our classes that one stitch seems to do beautifully with a particular color combination, whereas another stitch may look flat with the same colors. It is largely a matter of trial and error, and, of course, personal taste is also an important factor.

The Encroaching Gobelin is easy to compensate in large free areas. Even around a complex design it creates no problems, and its simple uniform appearance will not compete. The only difficulties with compensating are small "pockets" of canvas to be covered in and around a central motif.

The Encroaching Gobelin is perhaps not interesting enough to stand on its own. It might not do too well to cover an eyeglass case or an entire pillow with this stitch alone. In antique tapestries the Encroaching Gobelin Stitch was used to depict the actual design—hunting scenes, florals, landscapes, and so on—and it can, of course, be used in this way. But there the design itself held center stage, and not the stitch.

For subtle shading, a tight weave, and its own definitive look, the Encroaching Gobelin excels.

Luggage rack straps are done in Mosaic—outer border is a single row of Hungarian Point. The tiger pillow, designed by Sylvia Sidney, uses Encroaching Stitch. The unfinished wall hanging is worked in green background of Hungarian Point.

(See the photograph of doll's hair and of sky in brick cover done in Encroaching, pages 113, 229, also 115.) It moves quite quickly, affording a saving in time and number of stitches of over 50 percent when compared to the basic needlepoint stitch (BNS).

The Hungarian Ground Stitch

How to do the Hungarian Ground Stitch

This is a beautiful pattern. It is a bit more complex than the others, but well worth the effort of learning. We will use two colors for this square— a light and a dark. In this chapter green will be the light and blue the dark.

Thread up with three-ply Persian yarn in your light color first (green on the graphs). Select an available square (you are still saving your center and one corner square).

At this point it may be a good idea to review the concept of Main Line Hole and End Hole. The Main Line Hole is the hole through which your yarn and needle come to the front of the canvas. It changes with each stitch. Every time your yarn comes through to the front of the canvas, *that* hole it has just come through, is the Main Line Hole. On the other hand, every time your needle is inserted into the canvas, *that* hole is the End Hole. (Refer to Terms if this is not completely clear to you.) Remember these two terms; they will be helpful to you with this stitch, as well as with others later on.

Starting in the lower left-hand corner, pull your needle through to the front at the point where the two pencil lines meet.

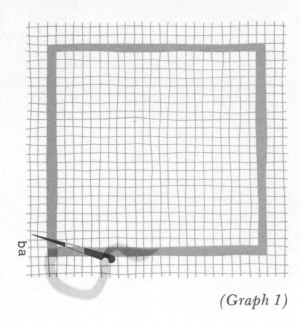

(Graph 1)

Work a straight stitch across four CATs to the right along track A and emerge on track B, one CAT in from the pencil line; that is, one CAT in from your Main Line Hole *(graph 1)*.

Again work a four-CAT stitch; since it *began* one CAT to the right of your previous Main Line Hole, it will now *extend* one CAT beyond and to the right of your End Hole.

In one motion emerge again on track C, now two CATs in from the pencil line, but again one CAT in from your Main Line Hole *(graph 2)*, and insert your needle across four CATs to the right. But this time your stitches will start moving back toward the pencil line and your needle will emerge on track D one CAT to the *left* of your Main Line Hole *(graph 3)*.

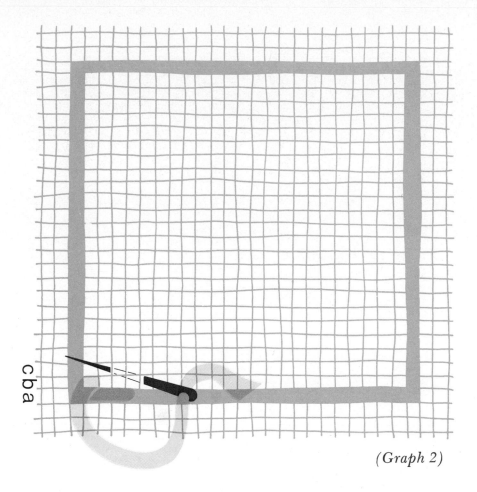

(Graph 2)

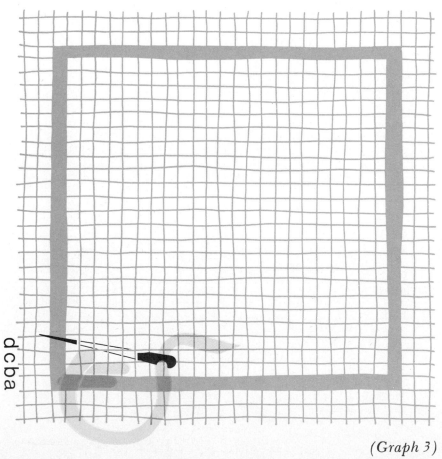

(Graph 3)

121

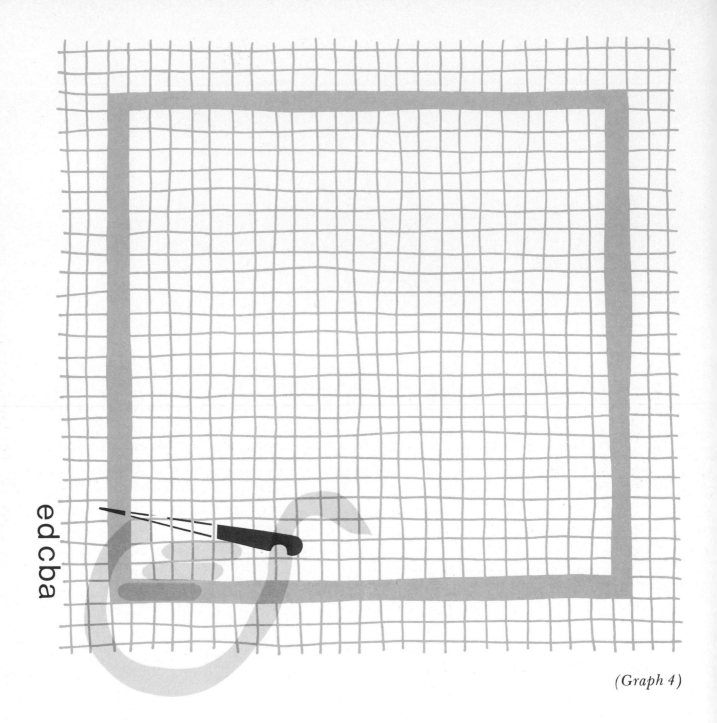

edcba

(Graph 4)

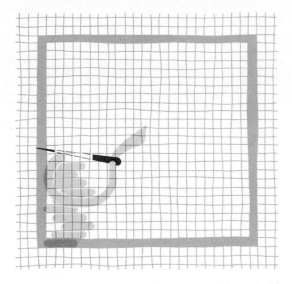

(Graph 5)

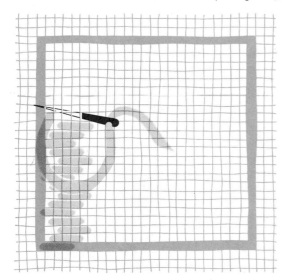

(Graph 6)

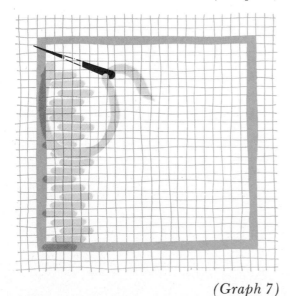

(Graph 7)

Remember, your Main Line Hole is the hole through which your yarn and needle come to the front of your canvas. It changes with each stitch, but when we refer to the Main Line Hole, we mean the *last* hole through which your yarn emerged.

You have just worked three four-CAT stitches, moving one CAT at a time to the right, and now you will reverse this process and start your stitches moving one CAT at a time to the left. Therefore, starting from a point one CAT to the left of your previous Main Line Hole, work a four-CAT stitch and emerge back on the pencil line on track E, ready to work another four-CAT stitch *(graph 4)*.

This tidal design is the Hungarian Ground pattern and it continues on in this way. After your base stitch on track A, it simply forms a pattern of two four-CAT stitches moving to the right and then two four-CAT stitches moving to the left. Every stitch in this tidal wave is the same size. If you are working it correctly, each stitch will extend one CAT beyond the previous stitch, or recede one CAT in from the previous stitch. A hint: your third stitch on track C is the furthest that any stitch will extend in this row, and all your outermost stitches should line up with it. If any stitches extend beyond it, you are making a mistake.

Continue this two-out, two-in pattern up to the top pencil line *(graphs 5, 6, 7)*.

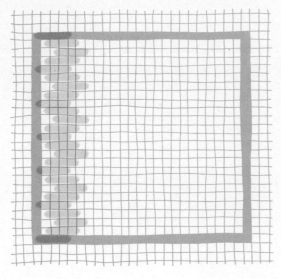

(Graph 8)

You should end evenly with a stitch that reaches into the upper left-hand corner at the juncture of the two pencil lines *(graph 8)*.

As you will be using the same color yarn for your second row, keep this strand in your needle. If you do not have enough to bother with, pull it through to the back, weave, and snip.

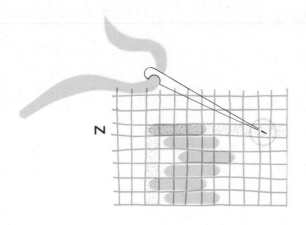

(Graph 9)

Let's start from the top for the second row. Count four CATS from the End Hole of your last stitch on the top pencil line *(graph 9)* and emerge with your needle on track Z *(graph 10)*. Be sure you have counted correctly. Work your stitch across four CATS to the right, insert, and move that "tide" to the left toward your first row. In other words, emerge with your needle one CAT to the left of your Main Line Hole *(graph 10)*. Work a four-CAT stitch, and emerge again on track Y, one CAT to the left of your Main Line Hole *(graph 11)*.

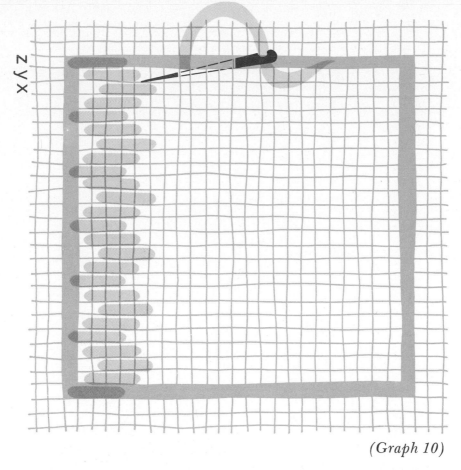

(Graph 10)

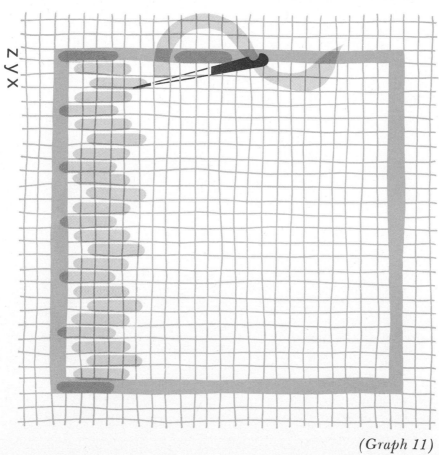

(Graph 11)

125

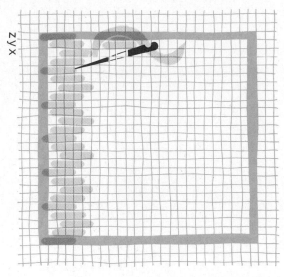

zyx

(Graph 12)

This stitch will share a hole with your previous row, and that will be the signal for your "tide" to start moving to the right *(graph 12)*.

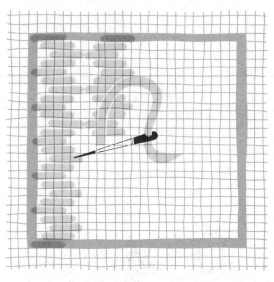

(Graph 13)

After that stitch on track X, continue to work two four-CAT stitches, moving to the right of your Main Line Hole one CAT at a time. Then move your "tide" back toward the previous row. In this manner, following the graphs *(graphs 13, 14)*, work a four-CAT stitch on every track as you go down the row, each stitch moving by only one CAT, either to the right or to the left. After the first stitch of your row, the pattern is simply two stitches out, two stitches back, two stitches out, two stitches back.

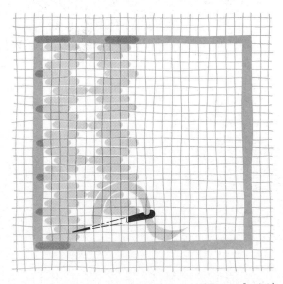

(Graph 14)

In the sauna: a rug of sample stitches, a vest and slipper in BNS and a turtle with Brick background. "Winning . . ." uses Brick around the "But," and the "Tennis Anyone?" racket cover has a Parisian background. The footstool is worked in alternate rows of Oblong Cross with Backstitch, Hungarian Point, Hungarian Ground and Old Florentine.

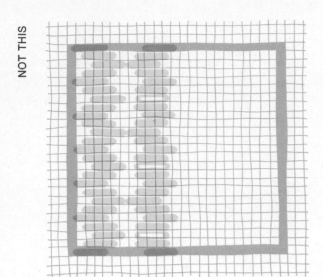

None of your stitches should start or end in the same place as the previous stitch (NOT THIS *graph 15*), and after the first stitch of each row, every fourth stitch should share a hole with the previous row (BUT THIS *graph 17*).

(Graph 15)

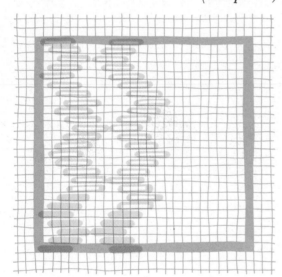

What could be easier? Well, for some people a lot of things could be easier I guess, and this stitch does demand a certain degree of concentration, even for those who learn very rapidly. I had a few students in one of my classes who got to chatting animatedly during the course of their lesson. They were having the best time together, and when I went to look at their work, it looked something like this (NOT THIS *graph 16*)!

(Graph 16)

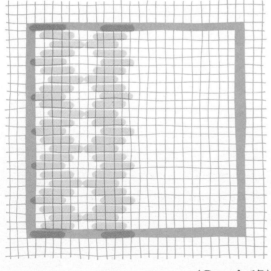

(Graph 17)

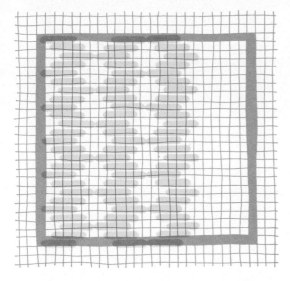

(Graph 18)

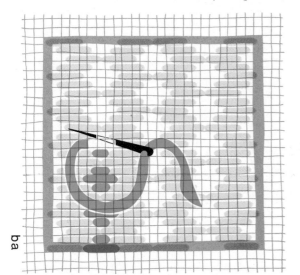

ba

(Graph 19)

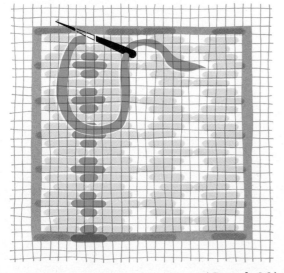

(Graph 20)

Your third row of "tide" will look just like your first. After the base stitch, it will move initially in the same direction as your first row, that is, to the right. It will start on the bottom, sharing a hole, and will begin the pattern of two stitches out and then two back *(graph 18)*, all the way up the row. You know you have made a mistake if after your first stitch your fourth stitches don't share holes with your previous row.

Work your "tides" right across the square, noticing that the "tides" in odd-numbered rows (first and third) move first to the right, while in even-numbered rows (second and fourth) the "tides" move first to the left. Another way of saying the same thing is to say that all even-numbered rows act alike, as do all odd-numbered rows. This may be important to you later on when you are experimenting with color.

When your rows are finished, you will be left with a neat pattern of diamond openings between the rows. Fill in these openings with your dark yarn, following the Hungarian Point pattern, which I assume you remember perfectly(!). But just in case your memory is a trifle fuzzy, I will provide a bit of a refresher.

Starting on row A on the lower left part of your square, emerge between your first and second tidal rows, sharing a hole with the first stitch of your first row. Work a straight four-CAT stitch to the right along the pencil line, emerge sharing a hole on track B, and work a two-CAT stitch to cover the exposed canvas *(graph 19)*.

Skip a track and begin a complete Hungarian diamond motif of two CAT–four CAT–two CAT stitches. You will naturally skip the row where your "tides" meet, and emerge ready to work another diamond motif *(graph 20)*.

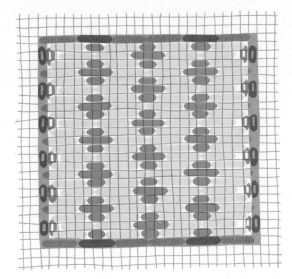

(Graph 21)

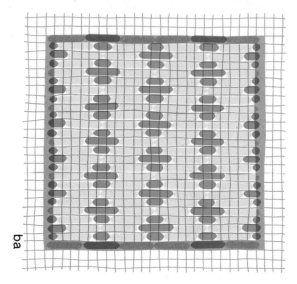

ba

(Graph 22)

You will compensate just as you did with the Hungarian Point pattern. Remember, this stitch is confusingly called the Hungarian *Ground*.

With your dark yarn, cover the canvas threads that are showing on either side of your square. On both the left and the right and starting on track B, form a half-diamond motif of one CAT, two CATS, one CAT, skip a row, and so on. Be sure that you do not get confused and work your stitches in the wrong direction as some people do occasionally. Your stitches, even these little ones, *always* go from left to right across a track (NOT THIS *graph 21*, BUT THIS *graph 22*). These little compensating points never need to touch the top or bottom pencil line, as those are already covered by your "tidal" rows. Remember, when you are working a one-CAT stitch, pull your yarn through to the back before emerging.

When you have finished this square, do two additional squares in the Hungarian Ground. This stitch adapts marvelously to a riot of colors. You might try, for instance, some of these ideas:

1. Work your tidal rows, as I have done, in one color, but work your little filler Hungarian Points in four colors in a set pattern—pale, medium, dark, darkest; pale, medium, dark, darkest, and so on.

2. Work your even-numbered tidal rows in one color, your odd-numbered rows in another color, and your filler stitches in a third color.

3. Work your first two tidal rows in one color and use a second color as filler. Then work your next two tidal rows in a third color and use a fourth color as filler.

4. Work your tidal rows in one color, and alternate your fillers in two other colors.

These are only a few of the many possibilities open to you. You are on your own. Let's see what you can come up with.

How, why and where to use the Hungarian Ground Stitch

This pattern does not compensate easily, but it stands beautifully on its own. It is so decorative that you can work up almost anything with it—eyeglass cases, slippers, tennis racket covers, pillows, rugs, pockets, covers for brick door stops, anything! It is not a terribly tight pattern, so if you are using it for something that will get a bit of wear, work it on a 14- or 16-mesh. It works up very quickly, and the results can be quite spectacular. It mixes beautifully with silk or rayon thread as well. The

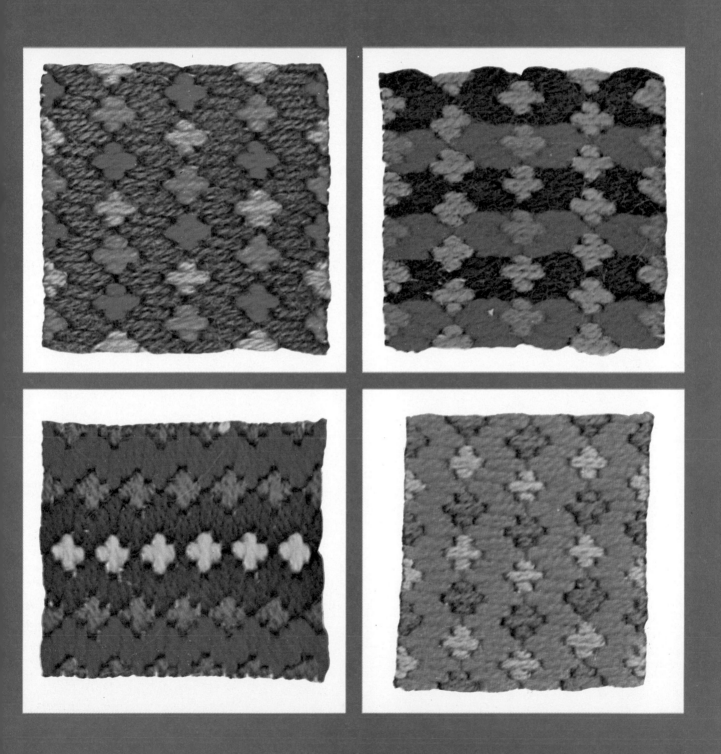

tidal rows might be wool and the fillers silk, cotton, or rayon to give added sheen and texture. You might want to try gold thread for the fillers.

Compared to the basic needlepoint stitch (BNS), it works up in about half the time. It *can* be used as background. As its name would suggest, it was used frequently as a "ground" stitch in earlier days. It has a great deal of movement to it, which adds dramatic impact to any canvas. When worked in one color only, it looks like lace (see the photo of the doll). Although it does not compensate easily, it is not impossible or even very difficult if you are able to keep a clear picture in your mind of the basic rhythm so that no matter how abbreviated it becomes, you are still working within that basic framework.

In the course of several years of running a needlepoint boutique, *In Stitches,* in Toronto, only two things have ever been "lifted." One was a lovely little eyeglass case worked in Hungarian Ground in maroons, greens, and ivory, and finished off with green velvet ribbon and a tiny bow at each side. I think it was taken because it was just irresistible. That is the highest compliment I can give the Hungarian Ground. Besides, I don't like to think evil of others.

For some mouth-watering samples of Hungarian Ground, see pages 47, 113, 127, 195, and 229.

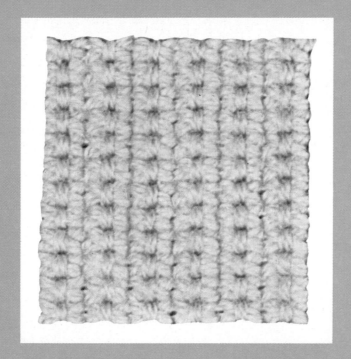

The Upright Cross with Back Stitch

How to do the Upright Cross with Back Stitch

The patterns we have learned thus far have differed, of course, but they have one basic similarity: They were all comprised of straight stitches, mostly four CATs long. In the next chapters, I will describe patterns that consist of *slanting* stitches and this is a key word. The stitches no longer move straight across a track from Main Line Hole to End Hole, but *slant* diagonally, usually from a lower left Main Line Hole to an upper right End Hole.

The Upright Cross pattern is one of the family of stitches called Cross Stitch patterns. There are many varieties of these, and this is a particularly lovely one.

This pattern is done in two parts. Use a light color for the first part—the Cross Stitch—and a dark color for the second part—the Back Stitch. In this chapter we use green for the light color and purple for the dark. Use full three-ply Persian yarn for the Cross Stitch, and only two ply for the Back Stitch. I will remind you of that later.

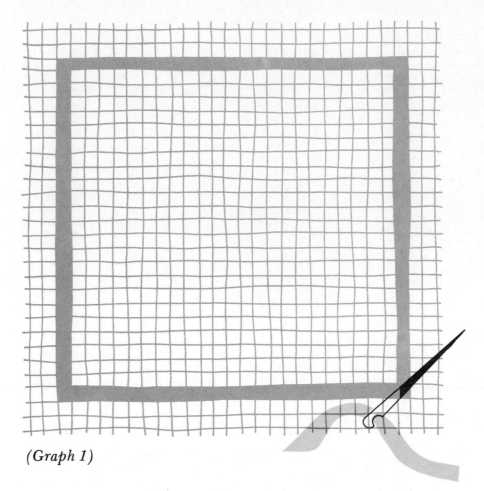

(Graph 1)

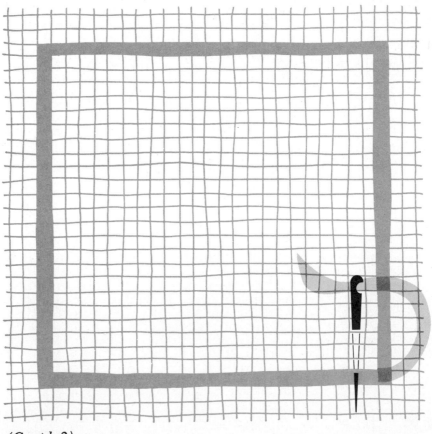

(Graph 2)

138

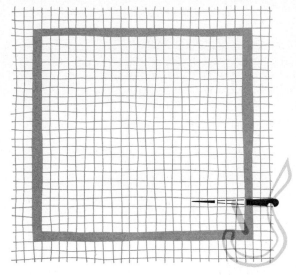

(Graph 3)

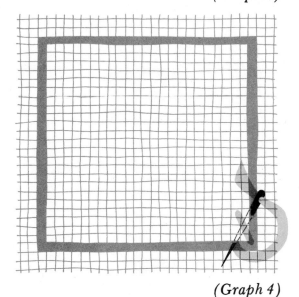

(Graph 4)

Thread your needle with three ply of light yarn and emerge to the front of your canvas in the lower *right*-hand corner of your square *(graph 1)*, at the juncture of the two pencil lines.

Count *up* four horizontal CATS and *left* two vertical CATS and insert your needle, emerging in one motion on your bottom pencil line on the same vertical track as your End Hole *(graph 2)*.

You have completed one leg of the X and are about to begin the second. Complete the second leg by working a stitch that crosses back over to the right-hand pencil line, four horizontal CATS up from the corner. Insert your needle and emerge back through your *previous Main Line Hole* (NOT THIS *graph 3*, BUT THIS *graph 4*).

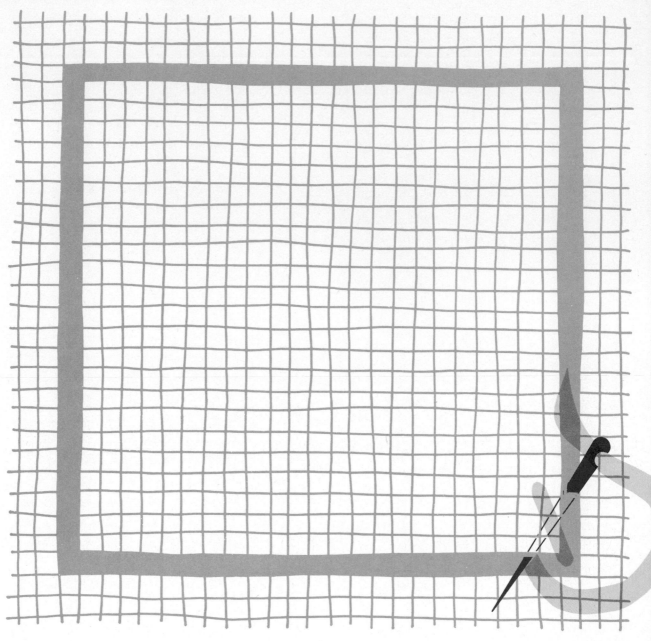

(Graph 5)

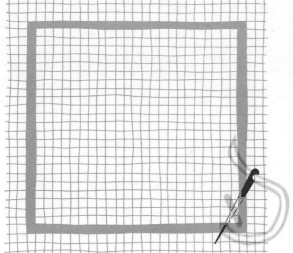

It is important to note that you are emerging through the hole you have just come out of, on the bottom pencil line *(graph 5)*.

As you share this hole, be careful not to split the yarn already in it or your stitches will not look neat (NOT THIS *graph 6,* BUT THIS *graph 7*).

(Graph 6)

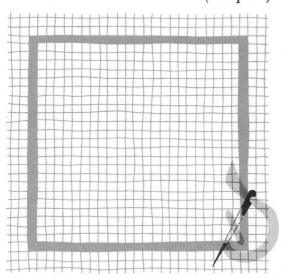

(Graph 7)

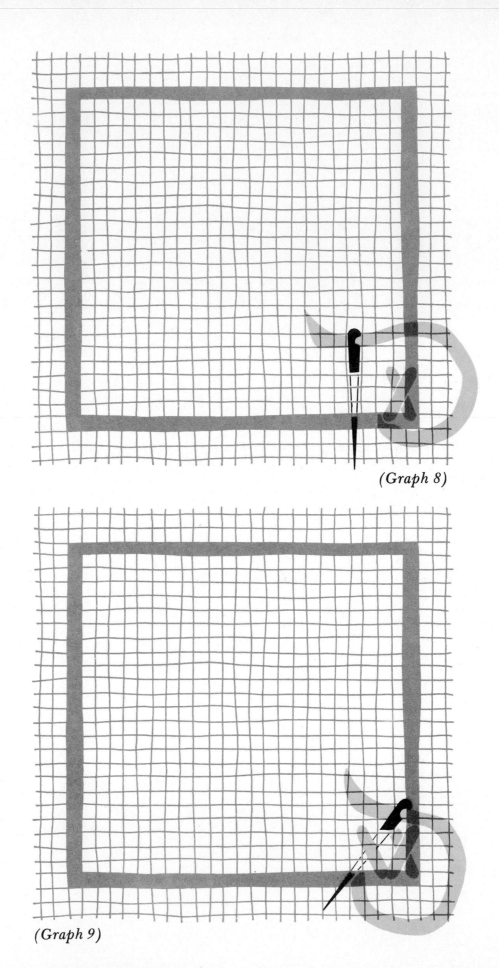

(Graph 8)

(Graph 9)

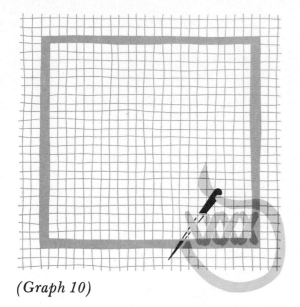

(Graph 10)

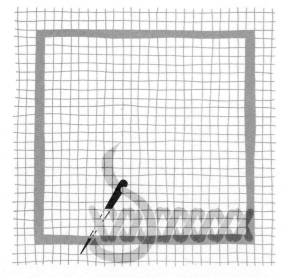

You have completed one X and are ready to start the next, which proceeds in the same fashion.

Reach up four horizontal CATS and left two vertical CATS and insert your needle, emerging on the bottom pencil line four horizontal CATS directly below your End Hole *(graph 8).*

You have one leg of another X completed, and from your present Main Line Hole, reach over to the right two CATS and up four CATS, sharing a hole with your first X, and emerging again through your present Main Line Hole on the bottom pencil line *(graph 9).* Pull the main line strand out of the way so that you can share that hole neatly.

Continue in this manner across the canvas until you reach the left-hand pencil line, which you should reach evenly with your final X *(graphs 10, 11, 12).*

(Graph 11)

(Graph 12)

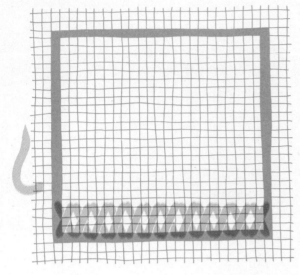

NOT THIS

(Graph 13)

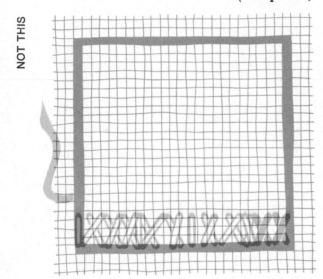

NOT THIS

(Graph 14)

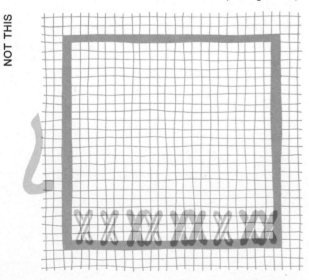

(Graph 15)

If you have not reached it evenly, you either miscounted when you originally ruled out your square or you made a mistake in working these stitches. Which is it? Do your stitches all move diagonally? Do they always move *up* four and *over* two (NOT THIS *graph 14*)? Did you always begin each X at the former Main Line Hole (NOR THIS *graph 15*, BUT THIS *graph 13*)? This is important because it is where most of the mistakes occur, particularly later on when the instructions are not fresh in your mind. Did you always remember to share a hole? For the correct look, check graph 13 again.

If your first row is properly completed, pull your leftover yarn forward to wait for you, and thread up with your dark yarn. Remember, it must be two ply if you are using Persian yarn, so peel one ply off.

It is in cases such as this that the versatility of the Persian yarn stands you in good stead, and this is one reason that I especially recommend it. The difference in weights and thickness makes your stitches more interesting, but this can also be achieved through judicious combinations of silk and rayon or cotton threads with your wool. Wool has the best wearing properties, so it is best to do the bulk of your work in wool, but later on do experiment with other weights and textures to get special effects.

With your two ply of dark yarn you are going to work a little belt around the waist of each of your X's. Emerge to the front of your canvas at the center point between your first two X's on your lower right *(graph 16)*. That is, two CATS up from the bottom pencil line and two CATS in from the right-hand pencil line.

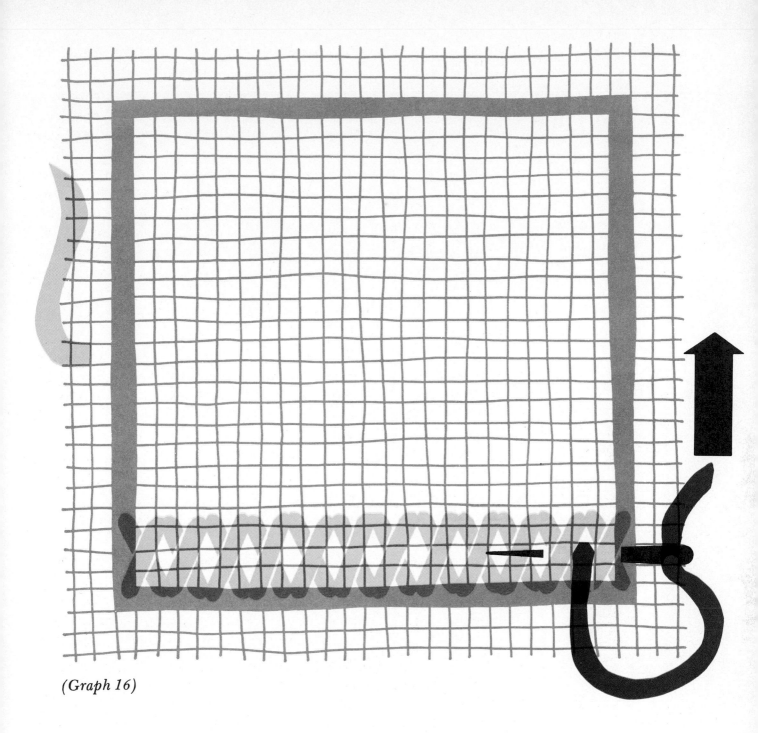

(Graph 16)

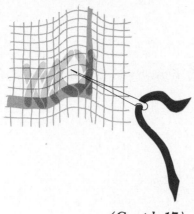

(Graph 17)

Your eye can usually tell you where to go without having to count. In any case, counting is difficult because the canvas is covered by your stitches. If you learn to bend your canvas slightly from top to bottom, just about where you think the hole should be, it will usually pop into view for you *(graph 17)*.

Work a two-CAT stitch to the *right,* across the waist of your first X, and emerge just to the *left* of your second X *(see graph 16),* that is, two CATS up and four CATS in.

As some yarns are fuzzier than others, depending on how they react to different dyes, you may find that the proper hole tries to elude you. But as I have said, if you bend your canvas lengthwise from top to bottom where you expect that hole to be, it will usually be forced to reveal itself.

Work another two-CAT nip at the waist of the second X, being sure to share a hole with the first Back Stitch, and reach behind your canvas to emerge just to the left of the next X in line *(graph 18).*

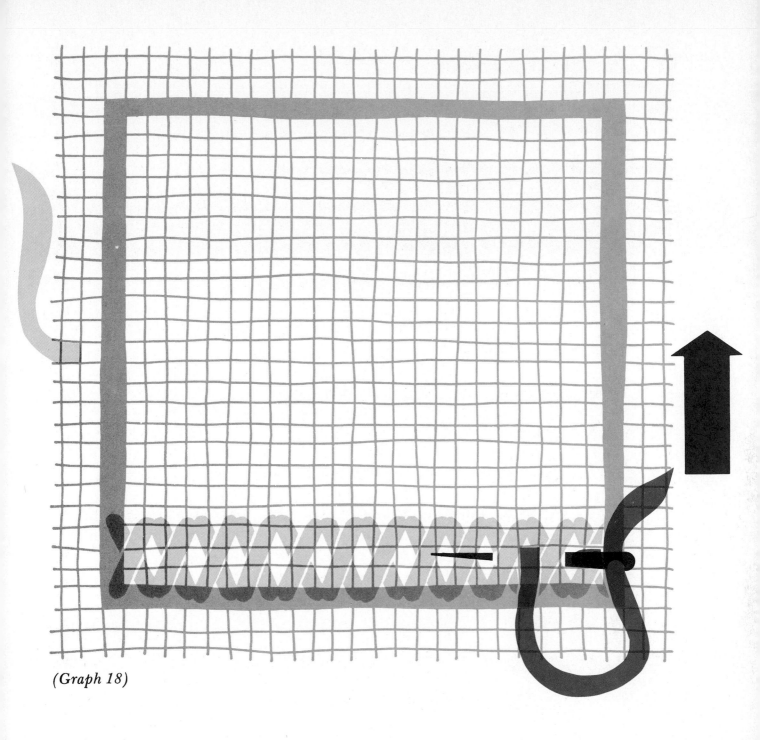

(Graph 18)

NOT THIS

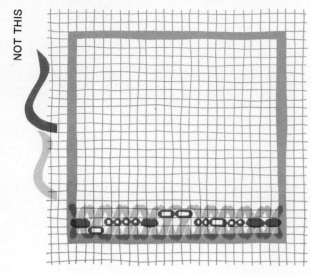

(Graph 19)

Be sure these little waist belts are straight across the middle of each X and that each one is two CATS, and not one CAT, long (NOT THIS *graph 19,* BUT THIS *graph 20*). Here, your eye will probably reveal a mistake *after* you have made it.

In order not to have to rip too far to fix a mistake, it's always a good idea to inspect your work frequently as you go along. Usually your eye will point out an error before an uneven ending does. But sometimes, even for me, it is hard to find a mistake that may be hidden in a nice fat stitch like this, and then only ripping will force it out into the open.

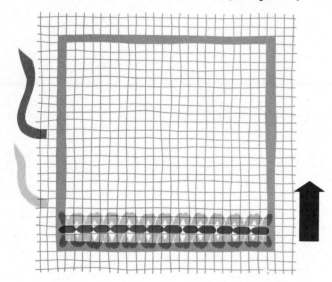

(Graph 20)

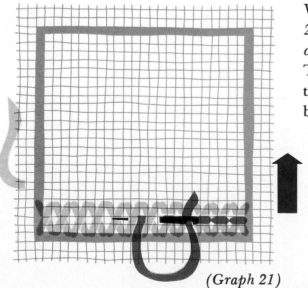

(Graph 21)

When you have "belted" all your X's *(graphs 20, 21, 22),* pull this yarn to the front and *turn your canvas upside down* to do the second row.
This stitch must be worked from right to left, and that is why you must turn your canvas before beginning the second row.

148

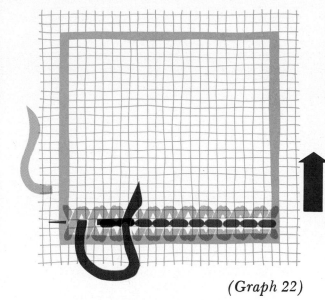

(Graph 22)

This may be a good time to point out another characteristic of Cross Stitches. You will notice that they are worked uniformly and in such a way that the *topmost* leg of the X always goes from lower left to upper right. You must not have a pattern of stitches in which some top legs point one way and some point the other. In general, the topmost leg of any Cross Stitch should ape the basic needlepoint stitch (BNS) and move from *lower left to upper right* (NOT THIS *graph 23*, BUT THIS *graph 24*). A good thing to remember, as we will need this bit of knowledge very soon.

NOT THIS

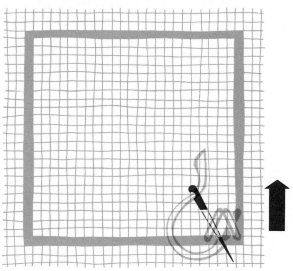

(Graph 23)

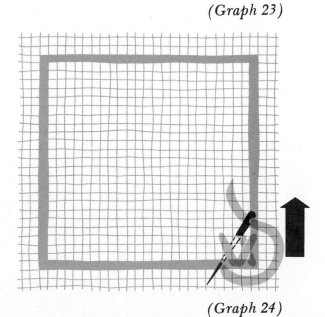

(Graph 24)

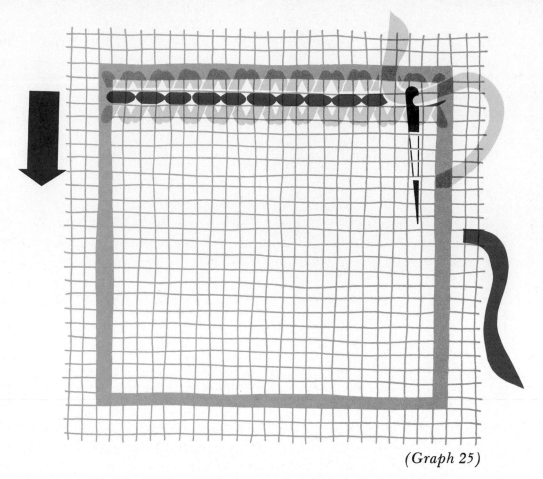

(Graph 25)

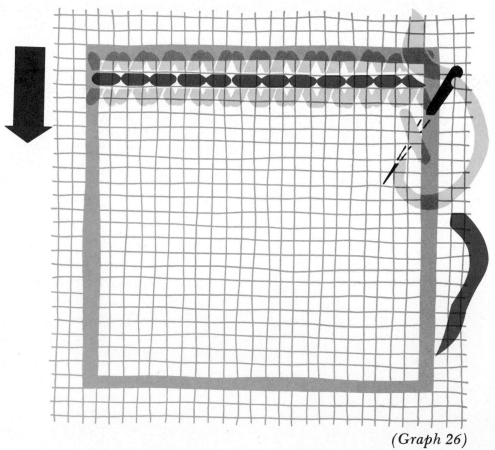

(Graph 26)

150

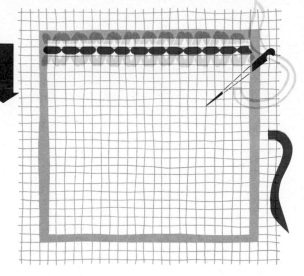

(Graph 27)

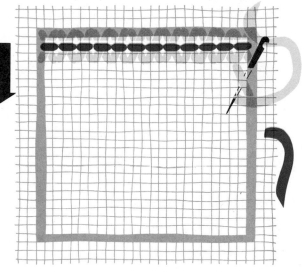

(Graph 28)

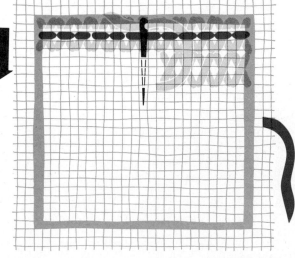

(Graph 29)

To proceed with the Upright Cross, pull your light-colored yarn through to the back and thread up.

From your first row, carefully count four CATS down on the right-hand pencil line, emerge, and reach up four CATS and left two CATS *(graph 25)* to insert your needle in a shared hole.

Emerge, as before, four horizontal CATS straight down on the same vertical track as your End Hole *(graph 25)*.

Insert your needle four CATS up and two CATS to the right on the right-hand pencil line, sharing a hole with your first row of X's.

Emerge through the Main Line Hole you have just vacated *(graph 26)*. This is the spot where most people go wrong, so don't join them. It may seem illogical to you to go right back to the hole you just came from, but that is what you do and that is where you start your next X (NOT THIS *graph 27*, BUT THIS *graph 28*).

This stitch pattern is not difficult once you have mastered the concept that after completing each X, you must go back through the hole from which you have just emerged. After mastering that, only the count may trip you up, but that is a fairly routine, mechanical thing. Just continue to execute X's that are four CATS high and two CATS wide all the way across your canvas *(graph 29)*.

If you run out of yarn during the course of a row, start up again with a new strand, either weaving it under some stitches at the back before you emerge,

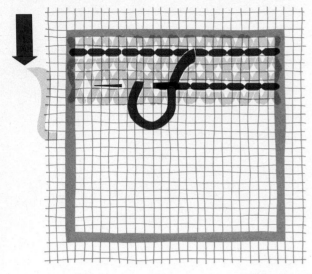

(Graph 30)

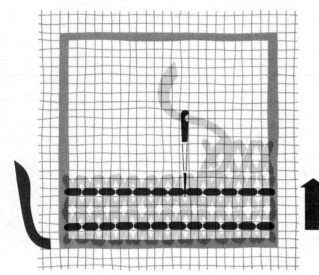

(Graph 31)

or holding a tail of yarn at the back in such a way that your first stitches will anchor it.

When the second row of X's is completed, bring your leftover yarn to the front, and pull your two-ply dark yarn to the back and thread up.

Still keeping your canvas upside down, complete this pattern by emerging as you did before, just to the left of the waist of the first X of this row, bending your canvas from top to bottom to find that hole *(graph 17)*. Work a small two-CAT nip at the waist—keep it loose—emerge just to the left of the next X, and so on *(graph 30)*.

For your third row, turn your canvas rightside up again and begin by sharing a hole on the right-hand pencil line and carrying on from there with the first leg of the X, moving four CATS up and two over *(graph 31)*. With each new row, you will turn the canvas so that you are always working from right to left on your square.

You may find that some canvas is showing between your rows, but that should block out later. Just keep your stitches loose, especially that nip at the waist.

This stitch needs no compensating as it will fit exactly into your square. But if, in your future endeavors, and I hope there will be many, you will use the Upright Cross with Back Stitch and find you have to compensate, you would simply make your X a bit smaller—perhaps only one CAT wide or three CATS high.

When you have finished this square, do two additional squares of Upright Cross with Back Stitch. Mix and match your Cross Stitches, using dark X's with light belts for one row and light X's with dark belts for the next; only remember that your X must always be three ply and the Back Stitch two ply, so you have to be careful about using leftover yarn. Try forming your X's into patterns of color, or use random colors. Once again, the key word is "imagination."

Any one mind, no matter how creative, can only come up with a certain number of ideas, so I am constantly examining my students' work and exclaiming over a new way of using a pattern that had never occurred to me. I am sure that the readers of this book will also invent new ways to use patterns, and I wish I could see them all.

How, why and where to use the Upright Cross with Back Stitch

Have you noticed that this pattern of stitches resembles smocking? Or sheaves of wheat? It is delicate and lovely in its own right, highly textured and susceptible to use in many colors. The X's can be turned horizontally on end and used in a design with vertical X's. It makes a lovely decorative stitch when used by itself for a small work, perhaps a jewel case or eyeglass case with a central square for an initial. It works extremely quickly, requiring only about 40 percent of the number of stitches that the basic needlepoint stitch (BNS) requires.

This pattern stands so high in texture that it does beautifully as a frame for a needlepoint design. Worked in about six or eight rows on all sides of a pillow or wall hanging, with a center motif done in a flat stitch, the basic needlepoint stitch for instance, it will stand out beautifully, giving a three dimensional effect to your work.

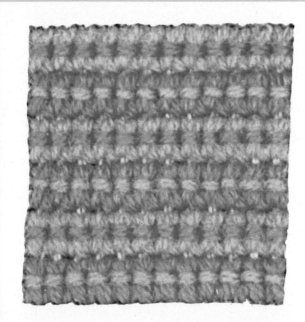

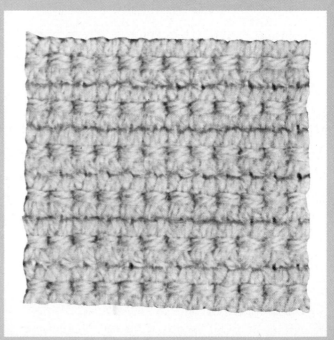

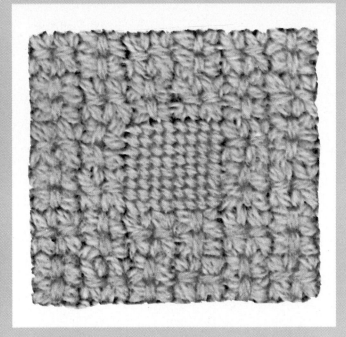

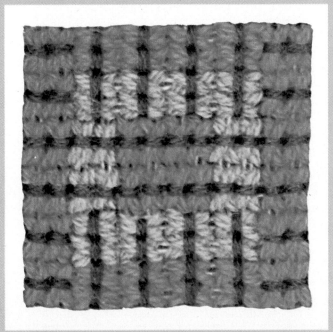

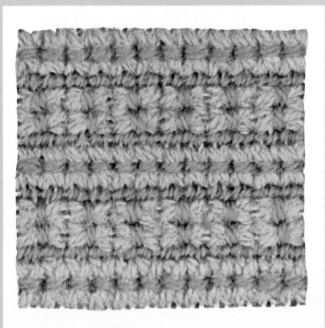

It compensates fairly easily, although the compensation does tend to change its appearance if stretched too far. Therefore, I do not recommend it for background if uneven borders are involved. It is a very decorative stitch and would prove to be competitive with most central designs. It is quite a loose stitch, and if it is to be used on an item that gets a good deal of wear, it would be best to use a 14- or 16-mesh canvas, but it is perfectly all right to use for a pillow or a wall hanging on 12-mesh canvas.

Turn to pages 3, 47, and 229 to see
how my students and I have used this lovely stitch.

LESSON
8

The
Mosaic
Stitch

We have arrived at the last of our decorative stitches, and being very different from the others, the Mosaic is a fine introduction to the basic needlepoint stitch (BNS), which will be described in all its forms and transmutations in the next few chapters.

With the Mosaic, we come to another designation: the slanted, or diagonal, stitch pattern. The Mosaic, although it resembles the Parisian, is worked with a diagonal stitch, and this is a good introduction to the basic needlepoint stitch (BNS).

Use all your colors for this stitch pattern, starting with your lightest and moving to the darkest, one step at a time. In this chapter we use gold, green, pink, blue, to purple in that order. Peel one ply off if you are using Persian yarn, as you will be using only *two ply* for the Mosaic. (Save the single plys that you peel off. Two single plys can be put together to form a double, so you do not waste yarn.)

To avoid confusion later on, let's go over some terms. The length of yarn coming up through a hole on the front of your canvas and ending with the needle is called the Main Line, and the hole from which it emerges is called the Main Line Hole (see Terms). Your Main Line Hole changes with each stitch you make, as it is always

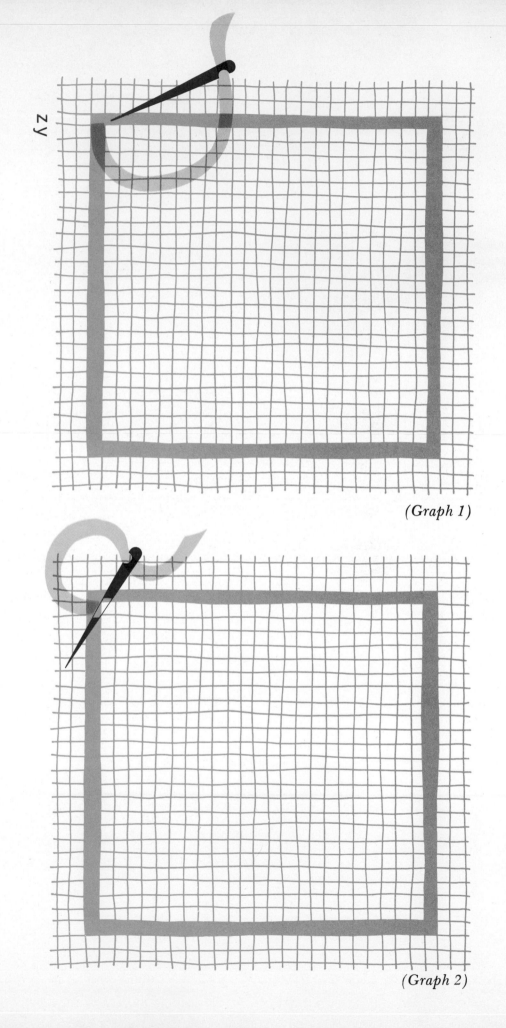

(Graph 1)

(Graph 2)

the hole through which your yarn extends to the front of the canvas. The hole into which you *insert* your needle through to the back of the canvas is your End Hole. That is easy to remember. Every individual stitch, then, begins with your needle emerging through the Main Line Hole and is completed when your needle is inserted into the End Hole. These labels are very important because I must give you what is basically a static word picture of a dynamic process that is constantly moving and changing; a one-dimensional description of a three-dimensional process. If you are clear on your labels, it is quite possible to say simply, "Emerge just below your Main Line Hole," and know that there can be no confusion. But if word meanings are confused, we are lost.

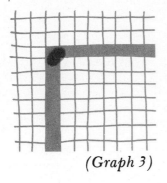

(Graph 3)

I still have a vivid memory of one of my earliest pupils struggling with a stitch during a class. Suddenly she looked up, eyes shining, "I finally understand, Mrs. Slater!" Very pleased, I asked her, "What helped you to understand?" I thought that perhaps I would learn some secret of communication. She gave me a smile of total victory as she divulged the key, "Well, I realize that when you say that all these stitches must *slant* . . ."
"Yes?" I urged her on. She finished eagerly, "You mean that all these stitches must *slant!*"

Words, words. Let's get their meanings very clear.

To begin the Mosaic Stitch, start almost in the upper left-hand corner on the left-hand pencil line, but one CAT down from the top of your square on track Y *(graph 1)*.

Work a small *diagonal* stitch up to the top pencil line *(graph 2)*. One hole, exactly in the corner, will be by-passed. This worries some people, but don't let it worry you; it will not show. Your stitch was worked up one CAT and over one CAT, crossing and covering one canvas intersection *(graph 3)*.

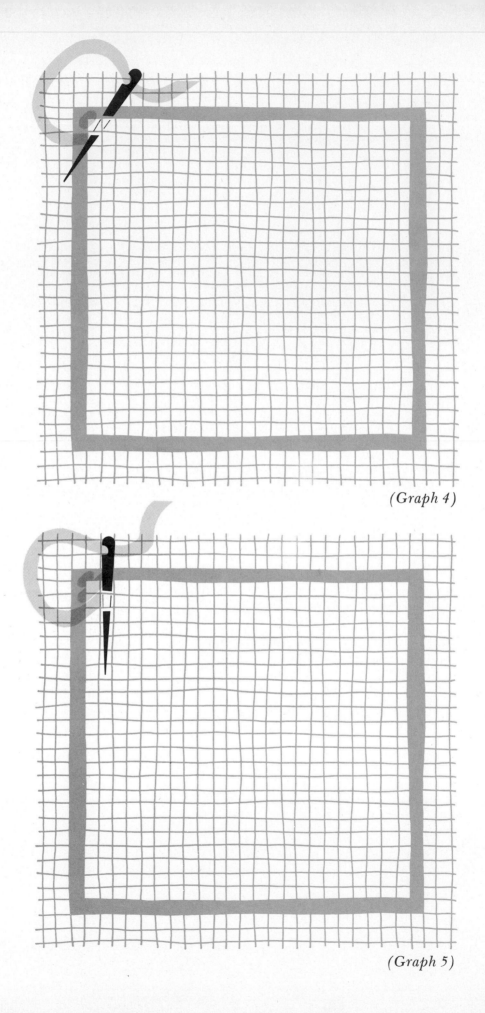

(Graph 4)

(Graph 5)

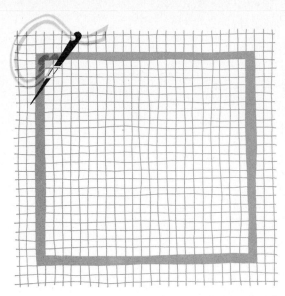

(Graph 6)

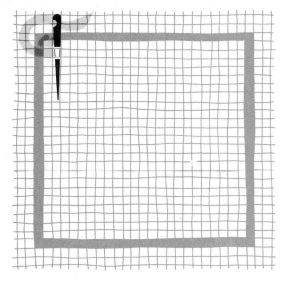

(Graph 7)

Emerge in one motion, directly under your Main Line Hole *(graph 2)*. Your second stitch is larger but also diagonal. It reaches back up to the top pencil line, right beside your previous End Hole, and emerges this time one CAT to the right of the previous Main Line Hole *(graph 4)*.

Insert just under your previous End Hole *(graph 5)*, and in preparation for your next little Mosaic motif, reach straight down the *back* of your canvas to emerge two CATS below your End Hole *(graph 5)*. Count those CATS carefully, and be sure to emerge two CATS *directly* below your End Hole, on the same track. "To be on the right track," is *very* important here. Don't get thrown off the track! (NOT THIS *graph 6,* BUT THIS *graph 7*).

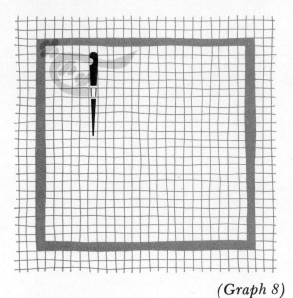

(Graph 8)

Now begin another Mosaic, consisting once again of a small diagonal stitch, a larger diagonal stitch, and a small diagonal stitch. Start by completing your first small diagonal stitch. Insert your needle so that it is both up one and over one canvas thread, crossing an intersection, emerge just *under* your Main Line, insert just to the right of your End Hole, emerge to the right of your Main Line Hole, insert just *under* your End Hole and now skip straight down the back of your canvas, two CATS under your End Hole, emerging in the *same track* as your End Hole. Remember to stay on the right track! See *graphs 8, 9, 10*.

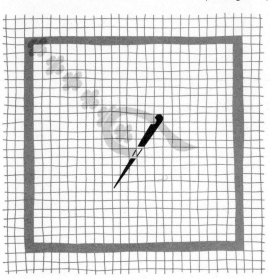

(Graph 9)

NOT THIS

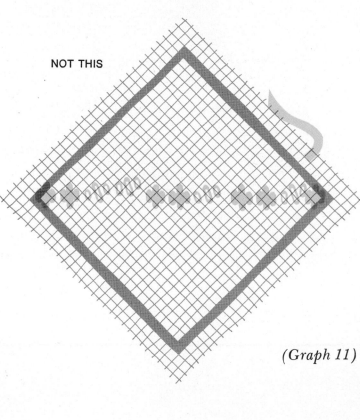

(Graph 11)

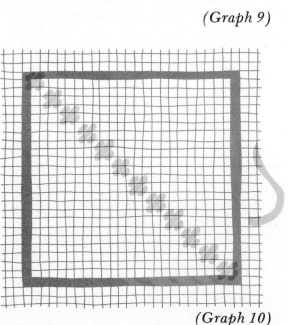

(Graph 10)

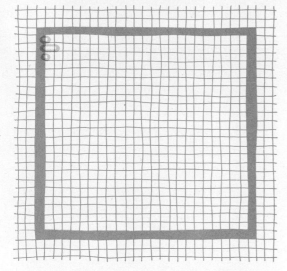

(Graph 12)

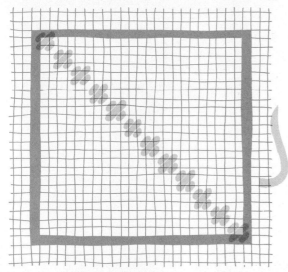

(Graph 13)

Once you understand the pattern of this little Mosaic, you will have no trouble, but I realize that so many words to describe something can make the quite simple seem difficult. After a few tries, I am sure you will get the pattern. That first little stitch is crucial because all the others follow from it. Therefore, be sure that it always slants, and in this regard, it is important that you hold your canvas straight in your lap, otherwise you won't be able to tell what is straight and what is slanted. Some of my pupils have a bad habit of holding their canvases *slanted* on their laps, and that makes for all kinds of trouble (NOT THIS *graph 11*). If your canvas is slanted, how can you gauge correctly if your stitch is straight (NOR THIS *graph 12*, BUT THIS *graph 13*)? Everything is relative, and your stitch has to be slanted relative to a straight canvas. Also, be sure that that first stitch of each Mosaic is as small as it can be; it should only cover one inter-section of canvas threads *(see graph 3)*.

I realize that for some people these additional explanations and analyses may be unnecessary, and sometimes even confusing. Once you feel you have the stitch pattern, just skim over the rest of the instructions in case there may be an important gem of wisdom or a dread warning hidden there. If you have mastered the pattern, it is not important that you try to follow each analysis. On the other hand, you may have the type of mind that needs to comprehend something thoroughly before you can proceed. If that is the case, read on carefully so that you know just what you will be doing before you attempt it.

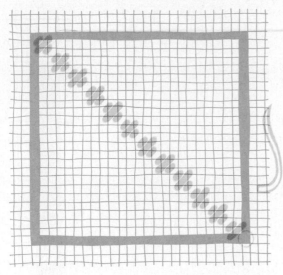

(Graph 14)

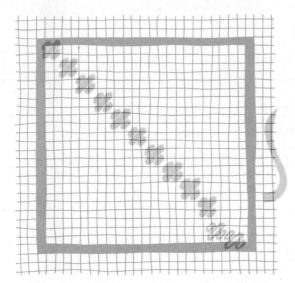

(Graph 15)

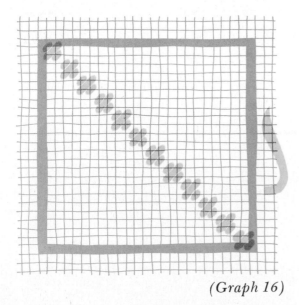

(Graph 16)

If you have been working the Mosaic correctly, you will finish your final Mosaic of the first row, neatly in the lower right-hand corner of your square. Don't get cold feet as so many do. Completely finish that last Mosaic with a small diagonal stitch which extends from the bottom pencil line up one CAT and over one CAT to the right-hand pencil line (NOT THIS *graph 14*). *Graph 17* shows you the correct route.

If you haven't ended correctly, was your square ruled properly? Can you see any errors as you look along that row? Does the line move evenly toward the right-hand corner (NOR THIS *graph 15*, BUT THIS *graph 16*)? Start ripping back; even if you don't see your error, it will probably show itself as you rip. Just let us hope that it wasn't there with the very first stitches!

When the first row is completed, bring your leftover yarn to the front of the canvas to wait for you, and thread up with your next lightest color in two ply.

Begin by emerging on the left-hand pencil line in the free hole under your first mosaic. Work your little slanting stitch, which will share a hole, and emerge *under* your Main Line Hole (*graph 17*).

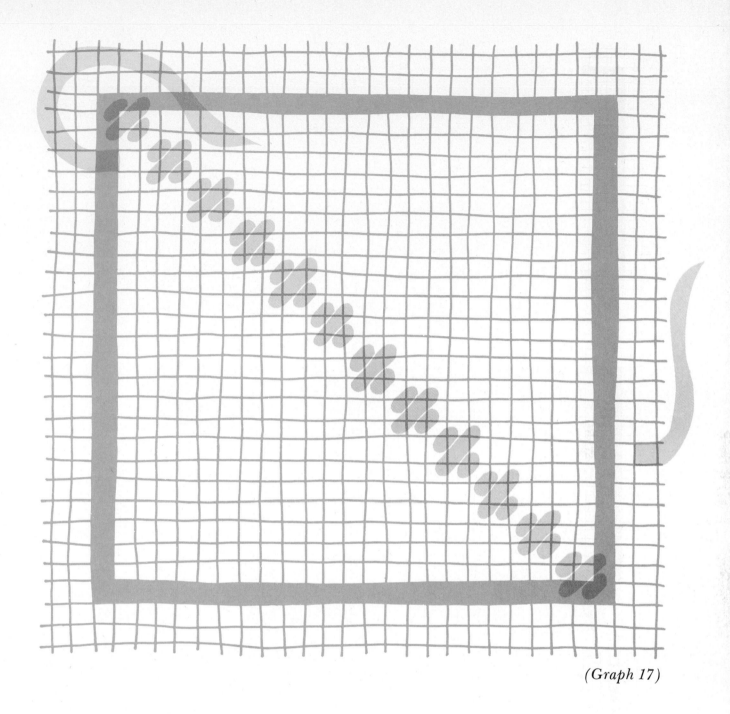

(Graph 17)

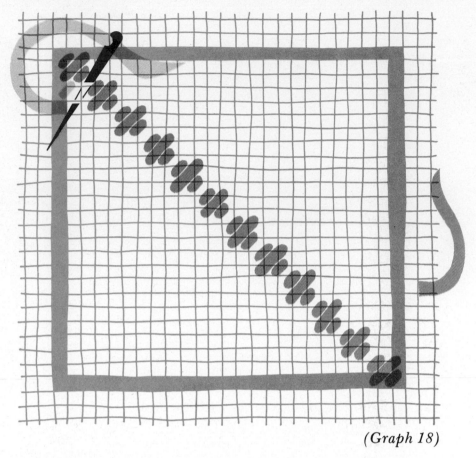

(Graph 18)

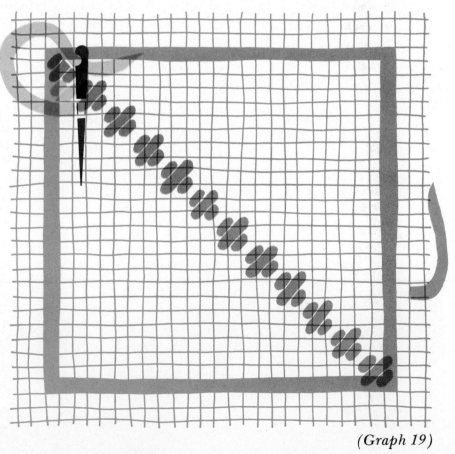

(Graph 19)

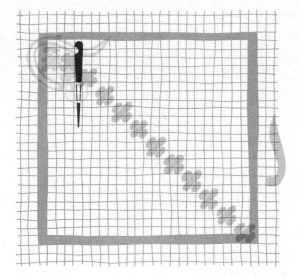

(Graph 20)

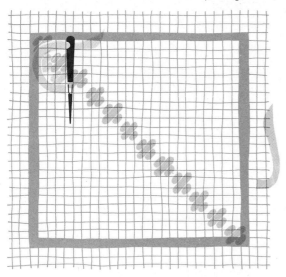

(Graph 21)

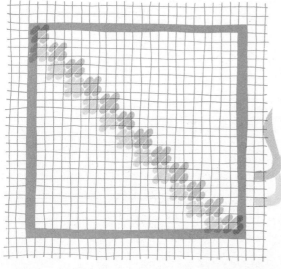

(Graph 22)

Insert to the *right* of your End Hole (this reaches in between two small Mosaics of your first row), emerge to the *right* of your Main Line Hole *(graph 18),* and insert *under* your End Hole *(graph 19).*

Now as before, bring your needle straight down the back of the canvas two CATS below your End Hole, on the same track, and you are ready to start another Mosaic motif *(graph 19).* Be sure not to reach mistakenly down *three* CATS, as one is hidden by your first row (NOT THIS *graph 20,* BUT THIS *graph 21*).

Once again let me caution you. It is that first small stitch that is the most crucial. Be sure it slants up to the right as it should *(graph 3).*

The second row also will end evenly on your bottom pencil line, snuggled up against your first row, with a completed Mosaic motif *(graph 22).*

As you complete each row, pull your leftover yarn forward and thread up with your next color in two ply, each time starting a new row in the first empty hole on the left-hand pencil line and working down diagonally.

When you have used all your five colors, it will be time to start up with your lightest yarn again. Pull the strand that is waiting for you at the bottom through to the back and thread up. We will now work the Mosaic from bottom to top.

Since student may begin any row either at top or bottom, *graphs 24, 25, 26, 27* show mosaics working upward in fifth or darkest shade for easier identification.

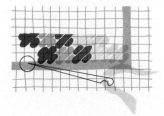

(Graph 23)

Weave your yarn through some stitches at the back of your canvas to where you will want to emerge . . . in the first empty hole on the bottom pencil line, just to the left of your last stitch of the previous row *(graph 23)*.

Work your small slanting stitch, which will share a hole, and as we are now moving up the row instead of down, we will simply reverse the previous process:

1. Work your first slanting stitch (it *always* slants up to the right).

2. Emerge immediately to the *left* of your Main Line Hole. Insert directly *over* your End Hole *(graphs 24 and 25)*.

3. Emerge over your Main Line Hole. Insert to the left of your End Hole.

4. Emerge two CATS to the *left* of your End Hole and *on the same track* and repeat step 1 *(graph 25)*.

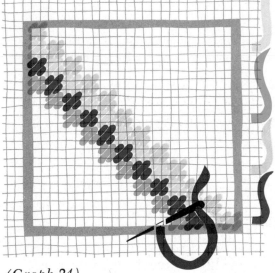

(Graph 24)

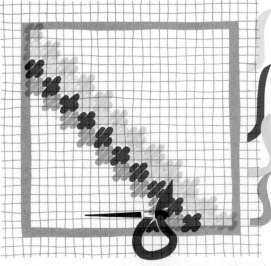

(Graph 25)

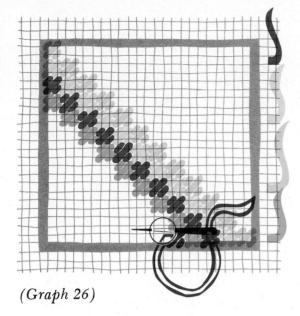

(Graph 26)

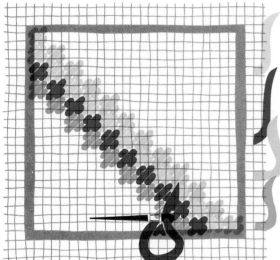

(Graph 27)

Be sure you emerge two CATS and not three CATS to the *left* of your End Hole as one CAT is hidden by your previous row and liable to be overlooked (NOT THIS *graph 26,* BUT THIS *graph 27*).

Working in this manner, you will end up evenly at the top of your row with a completed Mosaic. If you run out of yarn along the way, weave your short end under the back, snip off, and start with a new two-ply strand. There is a great temptation, as I have said elsewhere, to try to stretch a strand of yarn to finish a row or even finish one last Mosaic. Don't do it. It is a nuisance to have to thread up again for just one Mosaic, or sometimes for just one stitch! But resist the temptation to try to force the yarn to last. Take the time, make the effort, or else your stitches will show your impatience and much of your work will be wasted.

As you go from row to row, you will note that the diagonal rows keep getting shorter until you end up with just a single Mosaic at your lower left-hand corner. When this is done, turn your canvas upside down and start on the other half of your square. You can work your Mosaics from top to bottom or from bottom to top. You can even work the other half of your square *without* turning the canvas, but it is easier to turn the canvas, so I won't confuse you further. Perhaps you can figure it out for yourself if you think it worth the trouble.

For future reference, here is the key to the stitch pattern.

Top to Bottom

1. Work small slanting stitch.

2. Emerge *under* Main Line Hole. Insert *right* of End Hole.

3. Emerge *right* of Main Line Hole. Insert *under* End Hole.

4. Emerge two CATS straight down under End Hole and repeat.

Bottom to Top

1. Work small slanting stitch.

2. Emerge *left* of Main Line Hole. Insert *over* End Hole.

3. Emerge *over* Main Line Hole. Insert *left* of End Hole.

4. Emerge two CATS straight to the left of End Hole and repeat.

When you have completed this lovely square, do two additional squares in this pattern. It is, as I am sure you have already discovered, a delicately beautiful stitch, aptly named the Mosaic, as when it is worked in several colors as here, it resembles a mosaic. Worked in two colors, it becomes a checkerboard. Worked in yet another way, it becomes a modern Frank Stella type of design. You will have great fun with this stitch pattern.

How, why and where to use the Mosaic Stitch

The Mosaic is one of those stitch patterns that is good for just about anything. Its only drawback is that it saves you only 25 percent of the time and effort required to work the basic needlepoint stitch (BNS). Other patterns, as you have discovered, save you well over half the time required by the BNS. But for beauty and adaptability, this pattern has no equal. It

172

The rug is done in BNS. The seat cushion adds Mosaic and Parisian to BNS, and the Indian motif pillows are worked in Brick.

can stand alone, and even on 12-mesh canvas it is tight enough for almost any use. It compensates easily, falling back to a single BNS when there is not room for the larger diagonal, and therefore does very well as a background stitch worked all in one color or in soft, muted tones.

When the Mosaic is extended by one stitch, it becomes the Scotch Stitch, another very useful and popular pattern which saves a bit more time, but is not quite so easy to compensate or so tightly woven.

The lovely, delicate, and versatile Mosaic Stitch pattern, unlike the others, lies flat, so it will contrast well when used in combination with other decorative stitches to reveal a variety of textures.

Because of its neat little blocks, the Mosaic can form any number of beautiful arrangements of color and design, as you will see by studying the outpouring of ideas for the Mosaic squares demonstrated by my pupils. The photographs show just a few of them. Please don't feel that all the design possibilities have been exhausted by what you see here. They have not. *You* will create yet another if you try.

To get some good ideas, examine pages 3, 47, 92, 113, 114, 115, 173, and 229.

The BNS or Basic Needlepoint Stitch

How, why and where to use the the Basic Needlepoint Stitch

Have you noticed that the first six stitch patterns you did for your sampler are formed by straight or "Gobelin" stitches? This is one family of stitches. The next type you learned was a cross stitch, and there are dozens of variations in the cross stitch family. The Mosaic and now the BNS are diagonal stitches.

Many of the readers of this book have probably already done this stitch in one form or another. It is possible to work the Basic Needlepoint Stitch (BNS) according to several different methods, and they all look about the same on the *front* of the canvas.

"Then what difference does it make?" you may ask. "Why learn a new method? Why not just do it the easiest way and forget it?"

That is a fair question. Here is the answer. If *all* you care about is the *front* of the canvas, it doesn't matter which BNS you use. *But* there are other considerations, the most important being the wearing quality of your work. If you work many long hours on a piece of needlepoint, it would be a shame to have it wear thin. There are other considerations, too. How much does your canvas get pulled out of shape? How convenient is it to do the stitch this way? What speed can you attain? These are important points, and each method of doing the BNs will be considered in the light of these questions.

There are fundamentally three ways in which you can work your BNs. The Half Cross, which I do not teach here as I do not recommend it, provides no padding on the back of your canvas and therefore has very low wearing qualities. It should not be worked on a mono canvas, only on penelope, because the stress it places on the canvas pulls the canvas badly out of shape. It has to be turned upside down every other row, an inconvenience that slows you down considerably. And finally, there is a very slight but noticeable difference in the appearance of the stitch; it looks grosser, less delicately defined, than the others. Its assets? It is easy to learn and as it gives no padding at all, it uses the least amount of yarn. So much for the Half Cross.

Next is the Continental way of working the BNs. If I could only teach you *one* method, this would be the one I would teach. It is not the best, but it is the most versatile, and you must use the Continental form of BNs on just about every canvas to some degree. It is easy to learn, does nicely on a mono canvas such as we use, and gives a good solid padding to the back of the canvas.

"All right," you ask. "Then why not stop with the Continental and just learn that?" It pulls the canvas badly out of shape. A small item, a pillow for instance, can usually be blocked back into shape satisfactorily. But for a large work, such as a rug, a frame would have to be used in order to keep the canvas from becoming too distorted. I rarely recommend using a frame, as it restricts your mobility and slows you down

Needlepoint pillows add charm to a stark white sofa. The quickpoint Tiger Lily Pillow (in front) is worked in BNS. The orange and green geometric pillow is done in Brick background.

by half or more, because you cannot bring your needle to the front of the canvas in one motion.

In addition, when working the Continental you must keep turning your canvas upside down with each new row, and that is a terrible nuisance, as you will discover when you are working your initials or the date, which must be done in the Continental. Lastly, this stitch is just a bit less neat than the Basketweave.

Now we come to the Basketweave method. This is known as the method of experts and is used wherever there is a block of solid color, as opposed to a thin line of one color or scattered stitches here and there that must be done in the Continental. Why the Basketweave, especially since it is *not* learned quickly by most people? It pads the canvas beautifully. In fact, it gets its name from the handsome and solid basketweave pattern that is formed on the *back* of the canvas. It hardly pulls the canvas out of shape and has the additional quality of actually reinforcing the warp and woof of the canvas mesh as it is worked. The canvas need never be turned upside down, which is not only more convenient (you never know how many elbows you have until you start turning and dropping your yarns with each turn while squeezed on a plane or bus) but enables you to work faster. The Basketweave can be worked on mono canvas as well as penelope if petit point is desired, and although the difference is very, very slight, the stitches seem better articulated and finer on the front when done in this manner.

As with everything else in this world, it also has its drawbacks. What are they? It cannot be used on single lines of color or small intricate motifs that move this way and that without any solid block of one color. Furthermore, when used in one large open space, such as background, it tends to leave a faint diagonal line in places. It also uses a great deal of yarn, but that is because it is

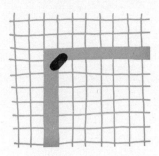

(Graph 1)

giving such a heavy padding to your work. The real drawback, and the only one that we need be concerned about, is that it is difficult to *teach*. Mind you, I do not contend that it is difficult to *do* because it isn't. It isn't even difficult to *learn* for many people, but to *teach?* That is another story.

This method should be mastered, and that's where my job begins. Your job is to cooperate by *using* the stitch as much as possible, so that it comes to you by rote after a while, a matter of mere instinct. Some people learn it, if not instantly, then fairly quickly. Others take longer, but remember, for what comfort it may afford, it is the teaching that is difficult, not the learning.

In addition to the catalog of BNS methods outlined above, there are a few others that are nameless because they are just adaptations of the others. For instance, one can work in the Continental method from top to bottom of your canvas instead of the usual right to left. There is also that indispensable "catch-as-catch-can" filler stitch that just darts here and there wherever the color yarn on your needle is called for, weaving under the stitches at the back to get the yarn to where it is needed. There is no pattern to that stitch. It just fills in wherever it must.

NOT THIS

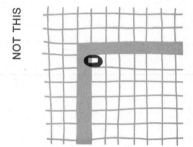

(Graph 2)

NOT THIS

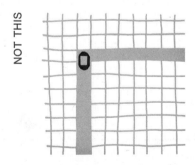

(Graph 3)

The one thing that every BNS stitch has in common is that it *slants* . . . and in a certain way. It slants from *lower left to upper right*. To say it another way, from your Main Line Hole, it slants up to the right, up one and over one canvas thread to your End Hole *(graph 1)*. It *always* slants, and it always covers a combination of only one vertical and one horizontal canvas thread. It manages that by slanting across one intersection of canvas threads. If the stitch does anything else—if it does not slant, slants in another direction, covers more than one intersection (NOT THIS *graph 2*, NOR THIS *graph 3*, NOR

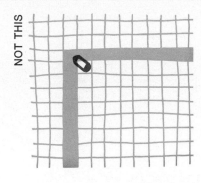

NOT THIS

(Graph 4)

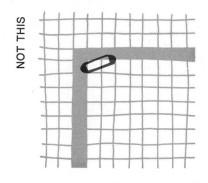

NOT THIS

(Graph 5)

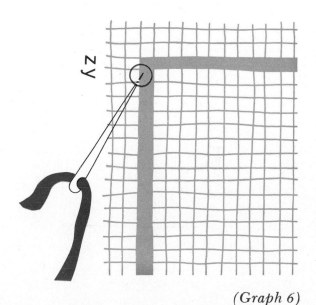

(Graph 6)

THIS *graph 4*, NOR THIS *graph 5*), or *whatever*
—it is not the BNS, the basic needlepoint stitch,
or Tent Stitch as it is also called *(see graph 1)*.
Like the Leaning Tower of Pisa, it always leans,
and in order for you to see that slant, be sure
to have your canvas sitting straight in your lap,
as I cautioned you with the Mosaic pattern.
Everything is relative, and if, an unlikely event
to be sure, you were hanging slanting in the
air, the Leaning Tower of Pisa might look straight
to you!

The proper way to work the Basketweave Stitch
is to start at the upper right-hand corner.
However, I am going to teach you first how to
do it from the upper left-hand corner. This is
not because I am inclined to be perverse, although
you may also find that to be true, but rather
because it is very difficult to start from the right,
and too many people tend to give up in despair
if taught that way from the outset. We will learn
to start correctly when you have already mastered
the pattern, and it will present much less of a
struggle. Fearful? Don't be. If I can do it, you
can. That's because I am *not* what you might
call a born needlewoman. I hate to sew. I cannot
thread a regular needle (as opposed to a tapestry
needle), and the original impetus for writing this
book came from my total frustration at trying
to follow a dress pattern with what seemed to me
to be woefully inadequate instructions, which
always assume that the reader has all sorts of
esoteric knowledge, of which I am not possessed.
So I decided to write a needlepoint book that
would assume nothing. I make no assumptions,
therefore, as we start to work on the Basketweave.

Thread up with two ply of yarn. A good rule to
remember is that slanting stitches use less yarn
than straight, or "Gobelin," stitches, hence only
two ply. You will be working in the corner

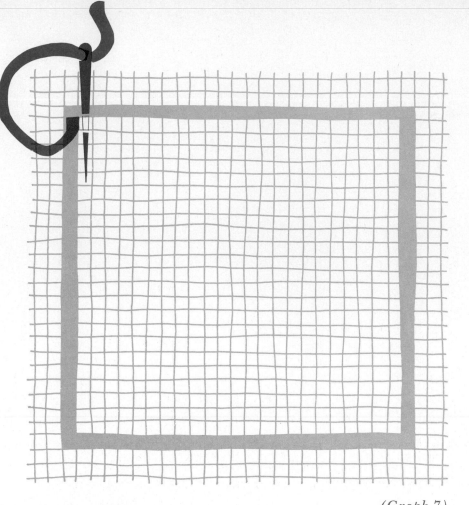

(Graph 7)

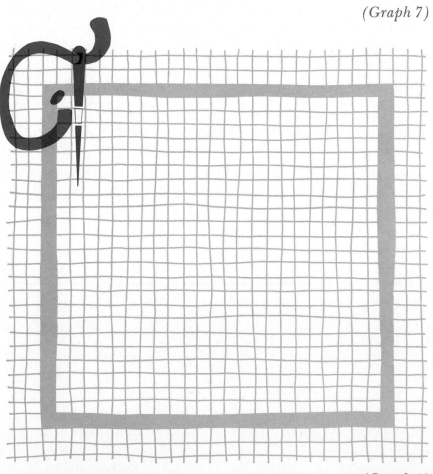

(Graph 8)

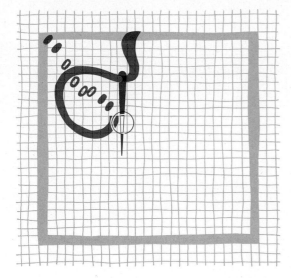

(Graph 9)

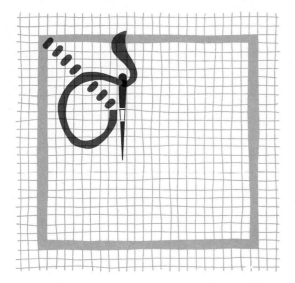

(Graph 10)

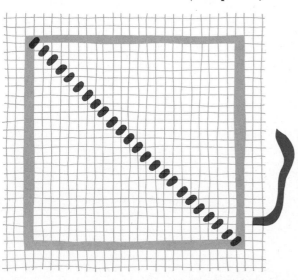

(Graph 11)

square that you have been saving, so use whatever color seems appropriate to balance your sampler from a color standpoint.

Begin, as with the Mosaic pattern, on the left-hand pencil line one CAT down from the corner on track Y (graph 6).

Insert on the top pencil line, one CAT to the right to work your small slanting BNS, and emerge two CATS straight down under your End Hole and on the same track (graph 7).

Work another small BNS and emerge again two CATS straight down under your End Hole (graph 8).

Don't be confused by the fact that while the BNS, the small slanting stitch on the front of your canvas, *always* slants up to the right, your needle on the *back* of your canvas reaches straight down below the End Hole before emerging again. It is simply that the stitch on the *front* of your canvas must slant. What goes on at the *back* of your canvas is a totally different matter. Don't confuse the two. Slant on the front; go straight on the back.

Continue on down in a diagonal line toward your lower right-hand corner. If you are working correctly, always picking up just two canvas threads, not one and not three, always reaching straight down from your End Hole before emerging (NOT THIS *graph 9,* BUT THIS *graph 10*), always . . . need I say it again, slanting the stitch and working it over just one intersection, then your reward will be that you will end up with your final stitch of the row slanting from the bottom pencil line up to the right-hand pencil line on track B (*graph 11*). I am assuming that if you ruled your canvas incorrectly, you surely would have discovered it by now and made the proper corrections.

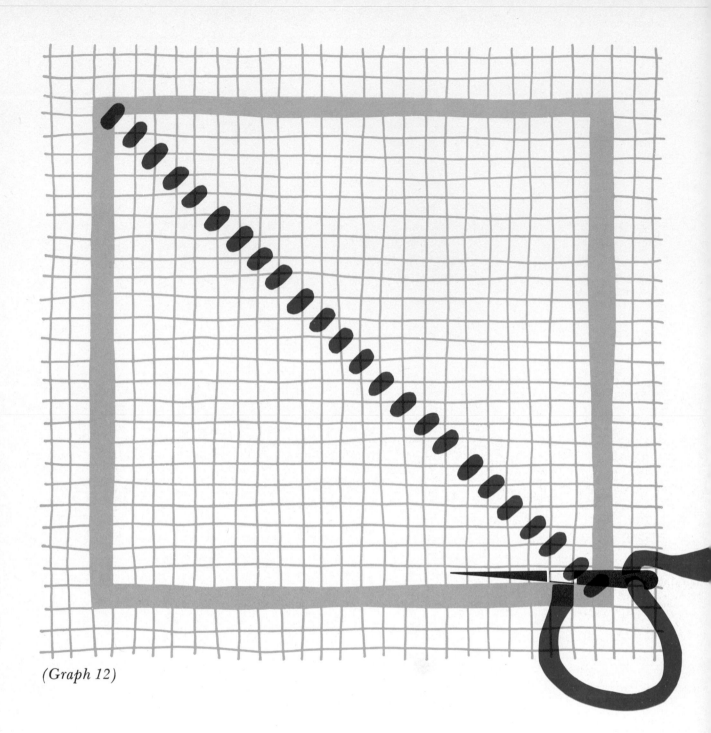

(Graph 12)

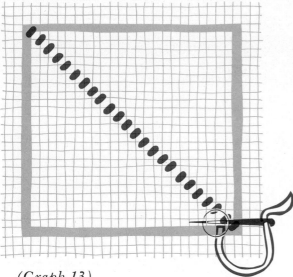

(Graph 13)

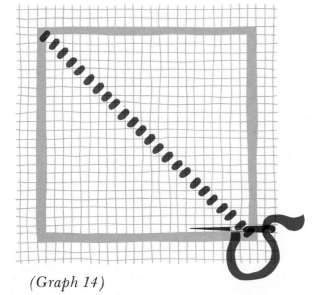

(Graph 14)

Complete the last stitch on the right-hand pencil line on track B, pull your yarn through to the back, and survey your work. You have completed one row of Basketweave. Not hard, was it?

The only difficulty with this stitch seems to come *right now* . . . when a row is completed. Where should you start your next row? The logical place, it seems to me, since you can't keep moving down, would be to come out on your bottom pencil line in the first hole to the left of your Main Line Hole. So emerge there *(graph 12),* and now we will work our way *up* the canvas in a diagonal line. (Actually, you have pretty much done it already with the Mosaic pattern.)

Work your small BNs, which will slant between stitches of your first row, and emerge two CATS directly to the *left* of your End Hole on the same track *(graph 12)*.

Count carefully because one of the CATS is covered by your first row of stitches and you may overlook it (NOT THIS! *graph 13,* BUT THIS *graph 14*).

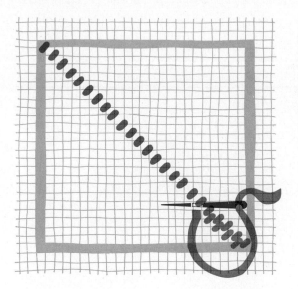

(Graph 15)

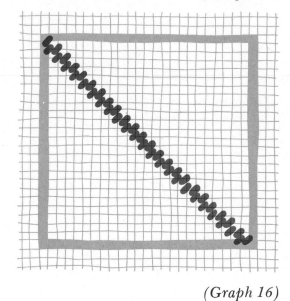

(Graph 16)

Actually, if you count the two CATS straight to the left of the End Hole properly, it will take you to the first empty hole on that track.

Emerge, work your BNS, emerge again two CATS straight to the left of your End Hole, and keep up this pattern all the way to the top *(graphs 15, 16)*.

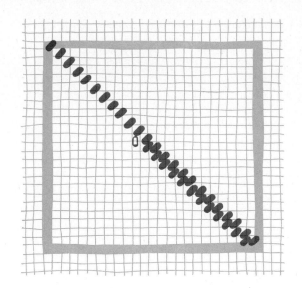

(Graph 17)

If you do not come out evenly, it is probably because you did not count those two CATS correctly *or* you did not make your stitches slant properly (NOT THIS *graph 17*, NOR THIS *graph 18*). Graph 15 shows the correct way.

When you reach the upper left pencil line, work that final BNS, pull your yarn through, and once again survey your work. You have finished two rows of Basketweave. It still seems easy, doesn't it? What do you do now?

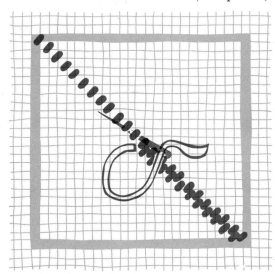

(Graph 18)

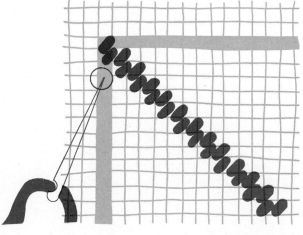

(Graph 19)

Again, it seems logical that since you cannot go on moving up because of the pencil line boundary, the best thing would be to come in on the left-hand pencil line in the first available hole under your Main Line Hole *(graph 19)*.

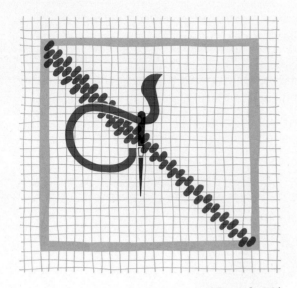

(Graph 20)

Emerge, work your BNs, and as you are now heading *down* your diagonal again, you reach *down* two CATs, straight under your End Hole as before, work your BNs, and emerge two CATs below your End Hole and so forth *(graph 20)*.

The secret to mastering this stitch lies in knowing what to do when you get to the end of a row. The rule is this: If you are moving *down* the diagonal, as your needle has been pointing you down all the way, check and see if you can start a new row by emerging down under your last Main Line Hole. If you can't, and you can't in this square because the pencil line will stop you, then simply emerge to the left of your Main Line Hole (NOT THIS *graph 21*, BUT THIS *graph 22*).

NOT THIS

(Graph 21)

(Graph 22)

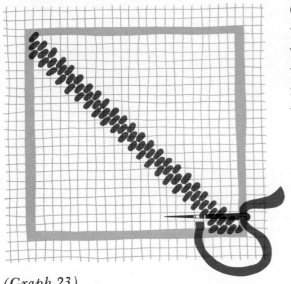

Caution: Do not start up your diagonal without doing this, or you will find you are missing a stitch on the bottom row. Work your BNS, pick up two CATS to the left, emerge ready to work the next BNS, and so forth all the way up *(graph 23)*.

(Graph 23)

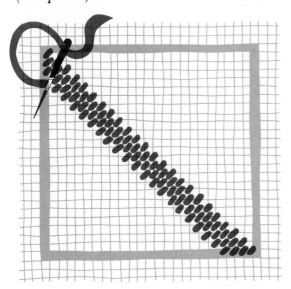

When you reach the *top* of any given row, as your needle has been pointing you *left*, check to see if you can move to the left of your Main Line Hole. In this square you cannot, unless you move beyond the boundaries of the square. Therefore, emerge *under* your last Main Line Hole *(graph 24)*.

The key is your last Main Line Hole. If you are quite clear on where and what that is, the rest should be easy. Going down a row, as your needle keeps moving *down* to emerge, you will check to see if you can start a new row *down* under your last Main Line Hole. If not, emerge to the left of it; that's simple. Moving *up* a row, as your needle keeps moving *left* two CATS to emerge again, check to see if you can start a new row by emerging to the *left* of your last Main Line Hole. If not, emerge under it. That's all there is to it.

(Graph 24)

(Graph 25)

You *must* finish each row completely before beginning the next row, and that's where many people go wrong. You will find stitches missing along your borders if you do not *finish* one row right to and including the pencil line and then *begin* your next row right *on* the pencil line again *(graphs 22, 25)*.

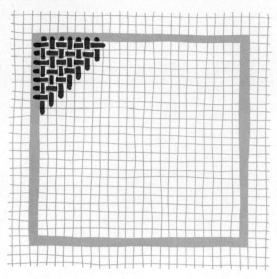

(Graph 26)

After you have worked three or four rows, turn your canvas over and look at the back to see the lovely Basketweave pattern that is forming. Some people do one square inside out in order to get that pattern on the front of the canvas. It is not easy because you have to figure out what to do with the loose ends. I'll leave that for the more courageous of you to discover for yourselves.

Complete the diagonal half of this square. If you run into problems, reread this chapter and consult the diagrams carefully. All the experts' hidden secrets lie therein.

A word of caution. If you put your work down for a while after fully completing a diagonal row, be sure when you pick it up again that your next row moves in the opposite direction or there will be a slight ridge where you went in the same direction twice consecutively. Check the reverse side, the pattern there will tell you if your last row was down (the stitches on the back will point downward) *(graph 26)* or up (the stitches on the back will point to the left). Some people prefer to end a line somewhere in the middle to be sure they start again correctly. After a while it will be easy for you to see from an uncompleted row where to begin and whether your steps were moving up or down.

You have now completed the lower diagonal half of your square. In the next chapter you will learn how to work the date in the upper half. Then simply work your Basketweave around the date. By that time you will know how to begin in the upper right-hand corner. But for the time being, leave this square unfinished.

Because your BNs must always slant up and to the right, as soon as you begin this stitch you establish a top and bottom to your square. From this point on you must no longer give your

Pale apricot sets off the sampler tote and sampler pillow at left. The needlepoint on the footstool is reproduced from an antique design. Fringed pillow has Brick background. The bellpull in four seasons motif is Bargello, the turtle a Maggie Lane design.

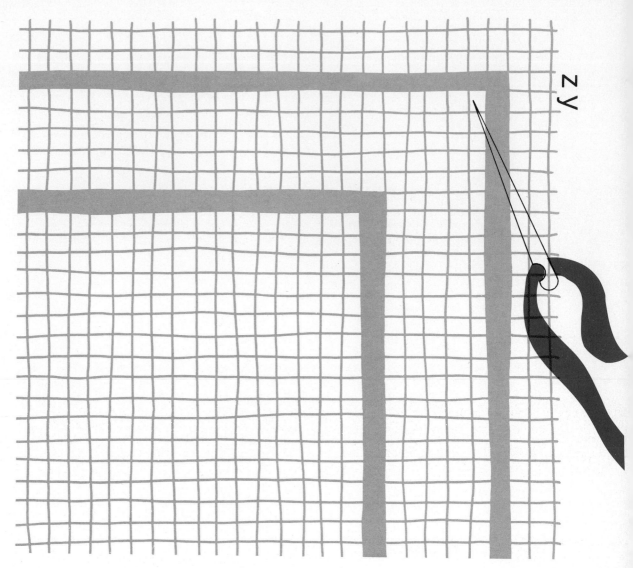

(Graph 27)

sampler a quarter turn or some of your stitches will face the wrong way. To be sure you don't make a mistake, it is a good idea to pencil an arrow pointing up along the side of your canvas so that when you are doing the Basketweave or any form of BNS, you will be sure to hold your canvas in the correct upright position. Upside down or right side up, your stitches look the same. But a quarter turn will send your entire canvas off kilter. Therefore, before you work on your initial or the date, as you will learn to do in the next chapter, pencil in your arrow pointing to the top.

Now I must teach you how to begin the Basketweave in the upper right-hand corner. If you comprehend the process of what we have been doing, it shouldn't be too difficult. I began your lesson in the left corner because I like beginners to start with a long diagonal line that runs down the middle of the square, so that they have time to master the stitch pattern. Once that pattern is mastered, the rest should be easier to explain.

Here we go. Thread up with two ply of yarn in your background color because now we are going to start on the background. It is quite amazing how your squares will stand out once you begin to surround them with needlepoint. In the upper right hand corner of your *sampler,* now, not of a square, emerge on track Y of your graph, one CAT in and one CAT down from your right-hand sampler corner *(graph 27).*

NOT THIS

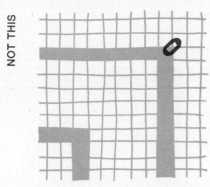

(Graph 28)

You would not, of course, start right *in* the upper right-hand corner at the juncture of the two pencil lincs, as then your little slanting stitch would slant right out of your sampler (NOT THIS *graph 28,* BUT THIS *graph 29*).

Work your small BNs right up into the corner and emerge just to the left of your Main Line Hole *(graph 30)*. We will now begin our first row *down* the diagonal. It will be a *very* short row, consisting of only two stitches, but don't let that throw you off.

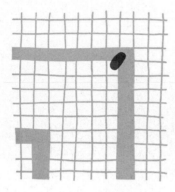

(Graph 29)

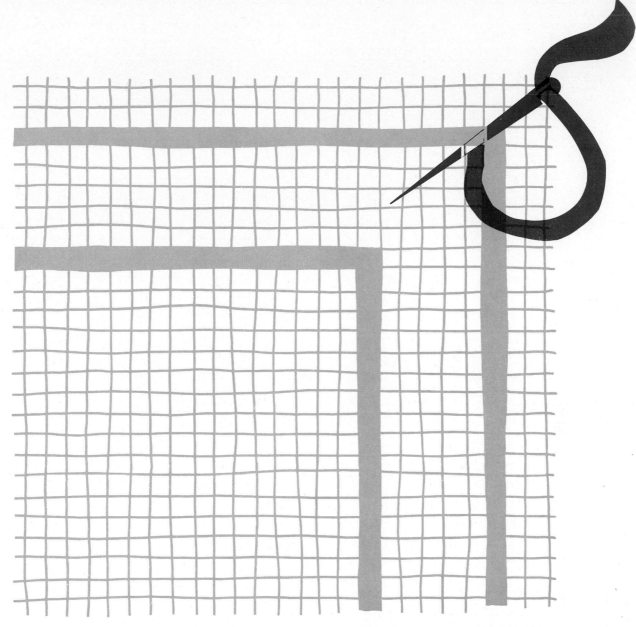

(Graph 30)

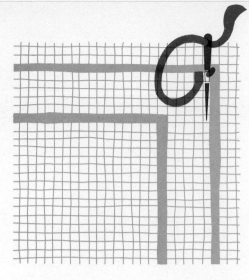

(Graph 31)

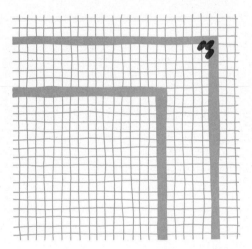

(Graph 32)

Work your small slanting BNs as before, reach *down* the back of your canvas two CATs, straight under your End Hole, and emerge *(graph 31)*. Work your BNs. You are at your border and can go no farther, so pull the yarn through to the back and survey your first row *(graph 32)*.

Where do you start the next row upward? The rule is, when moving *down* a diagonal (when the needle points down), check to see if you can emerge *down* under your Main Line Hole without going outside your boundaries. Yes, indeed you can this time.

Therefore, emerge *down* under your previous Main Line Hole *(graph 33)* in order to start your next row upward. This row too will be very short, but don't lose sight of the direction, which is now upward.

Work a BNs which touches the right-hand pencil line again *(graph 33)*.

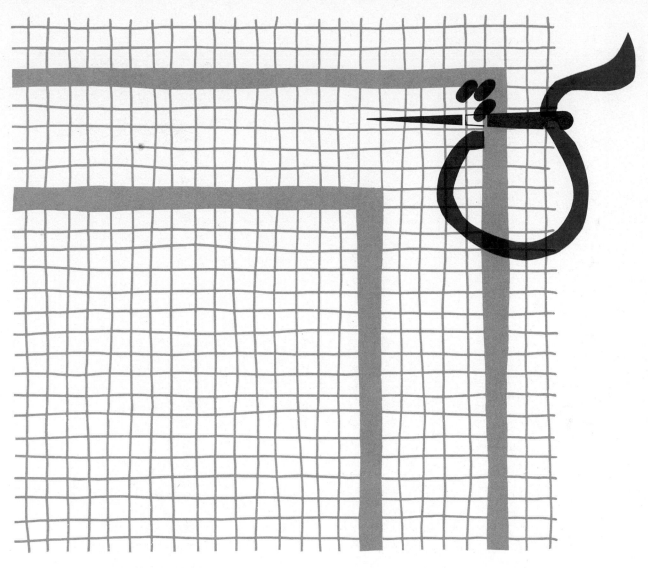

(Graph 33)

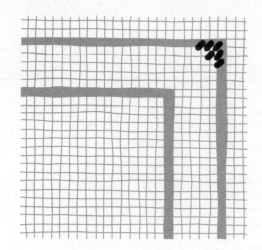

(Graph 34)

Reach two CATS straight to the left of your End Hole, work a BNS, reach two CATS straight to the left of the End Hole, and work a BNS which this time is going to touch your upper border, so pull it through to survey the second row *(graph 34)*.

We are now ready to begin our next row down. What is the rule? When moving upward our needle has always emerged to the *left* and therefore we must check to see if we can begin the next row by moving to the *left* of our Main Line Hole. If so, we will do it. As it turns out, we can indeed, emerge to the left of our Main Line Hole, so we do *(graph 35)*. Then we work our BNS and reach two CATS straight down under the new End Hole, and so on, heading down the diagonal.

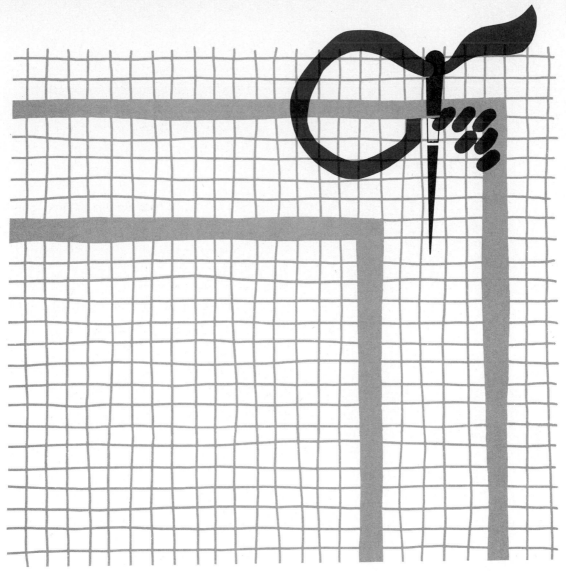

(Graph 35)

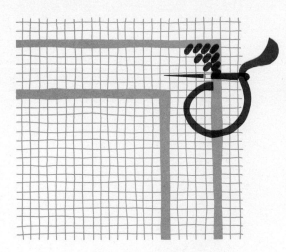
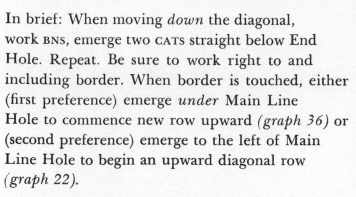

In brief: When moving *down* the diagonal, work BNS, emerge two CATS straight below End Hole. Repeat. Be sure to work right to and including border. When border is touched, either (first preference) emerge *under* Main Line Hole to commence new row upward *(graph 36)* or (second preference) emerge to the left of Main Line Hole to begin an upward diagonal row *(graph 22)*.

(Graph 36)

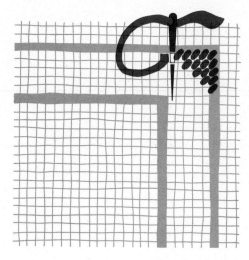

When moving *up* the diagonal, work BNS and emerge two CATS straight to the left of End Hole. Repeat. When upper border is touched (be sure last stitch touches the border before starting next row), either (first preference) emerge to the *left* of Main Line Hole to begin the row downward *(graph 37)* or (second preference) emerge under Main Line Hole to begin the next row downward *(graph 25)*.

(Graph 37)

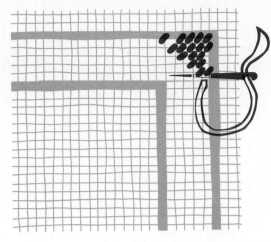

(Graph 38)

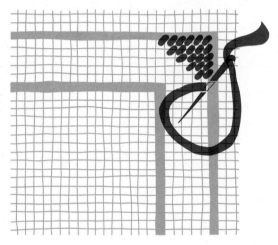

(Graph 39)

That is all there is to it. One last caution: Be sure that you end each row by going right to and including the border; otherwise you may find yourself heading back before you have completed the entire row. In fact, as you may have noticed, you touch that border twice. That is to say, you touch the border to finish a row, and you touch it again to start your next row. How else would you have stitches running along your border? It is a common mistake of beginners to the Basketweave Stitch to miss those stitches along the border (NOT THIS *graph 38*, BUT THIS *graph 39*), and they don't know what they are doing wrong. They are forgetting that they have not finished one row until they touch the border, and they can't head back again unless they touch it again.

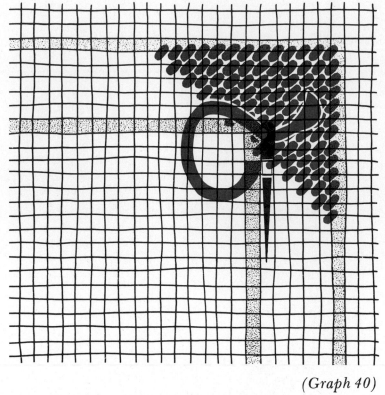

(Graph 40)

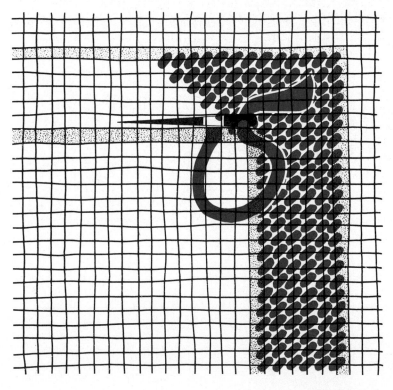

(Graph 41)

206

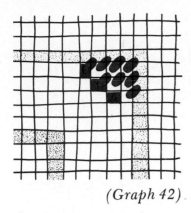

(Graph 42)

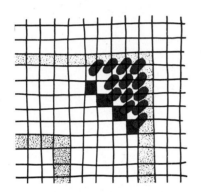

(Graph 43)

Now continue your up and down diagonals as long as you can. When the square gets in your way and you cannot continue *up* your diagonal, that is, you can no longer reach two CATS to the left without going *into* your square, then simply follow your rules: reach *under* your Main Line Hole and start down again *(graph 40)*. Be sure to stitch right on your pencil lines, sharing the hole with the stitches in the square.

Continue with your up and down diagonals along the right edge of your sampler. You should not have a *straight line* until you reach the very bottom. When you have reached the bottom of your sampler, you might decide to pick up along the top border. If your last row was a down diagonal, you will start now with an up diagonal. You had reached the pencil line top of your square and can now go down no further, so remember your rules: on a downward swing reach under your Main Line if you can; if *not* (as now), emerge *next to* your Main Line Hole with a BNS and start your next row up *(graph 41)*.

I haven't told you what to do when you run out of your strand of yarn, as I assume that you know to pull the leftover bit through to the back, weave it under, and snip it off. But I promised not to make assumptions, and it may sometimes be a bit difficult at first, when doing the Basketweave, to see where to emerge again after you have lost the momentum of your pattern. Notice that your diagonals move in steps. You must start in such a way as to complete the next step. If it was a *downward* diagonal, locate your last stitch of that row and emerge two CATS under its End Hole *(graph 42)*. If it was an upward diagonal, emerge two CATS to the left of the End Hole of your last stitch *(graph 43)*.

I keep repeating things I know, particularly the most important points, but that is because I have so frequently found that words mean different things to different people, and saying a thing one way may draw a blank from someone, who, when the same thing is explained differently, will comprehend instantly. So I try to say things in a few different ways to be sure I catch everyone in my net. If you have understood the first time round, don't feel I am being condescending. On another point, you may appreciate the multiple explanations.

There is so much to learn at first that it can be difficult to absorb all the bits of information that I throw at you. You may remember some, at once. But don't be irritated by the redundancy, as I suspect that sooner or later everyone will welcome its repetition, perhaps not even realizing that he or she missed it the first time round.

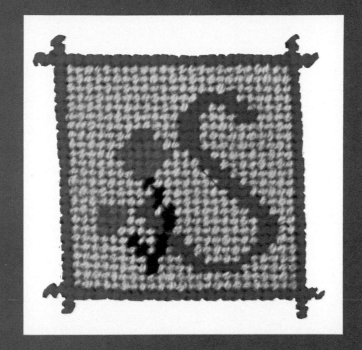

The Continental pattern of the BNS

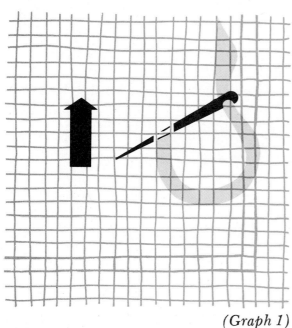

(Graph 1)

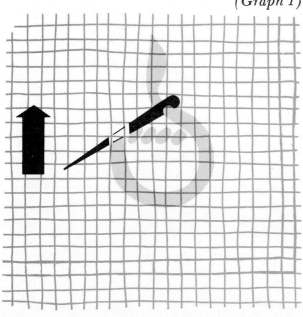

How to do the Continental pattern of the BNS

I am sure the Continental is easier to do than the dance step of the same name. At least for me.

Practice the Continental *outside* your sampler boundaries only, as I would not want any blocks of Continental done within the sampler. Once you learn it, you will be able to use this stitch and the catch-as-catch-can filler stitch to work your initial in the center square and the date in the open diagonal half of your corner square.

Thread up with any color, as this is practice only. We only use two ply for the various BNS's on this 12-mesh.

Come through to the front of your canvas anywhere outside of the penciled border of your sampler *(graph 1)*. Work a small BNS and emerge to the left of your Main Line Hole, work a BNS, emerge to the left of your Main Line Hole, work a BNS, and so on *(graph 2)*. It is quite easy. Just work this pattern for about ten stitches, pull your yarn through to the back, and turn your canvas upside down.

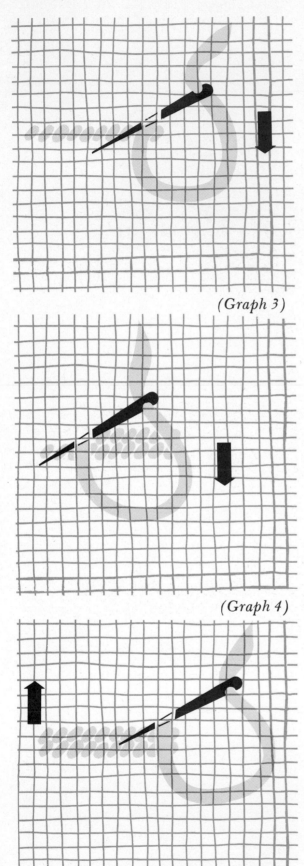

(Graph 3)

(Graph 4)

(Graph 5)

Bring your needle through to the front, just over what was your last End Hole when your canvas was right side up, share the hole, work your small slanting BNs up to the right, emerge to the left of your Main Line Hole, *(graph 3)* share a hole, work a BNs, and emerge to the left of your Main Line Hole, and so on *(graph 4)*.

Continue until you have worked another ten stitches, pull your yarn through, and turn your canvas right side up again *(graph 5)*.

A gift to a writer, who lives by the "word," this pillow uses a variation of Brick Stitch with the sky worked in Parisian.

At top right, floral pillow with Parisian background. Partially obscured, at bottom right, framed, Audubon's Snow Goose, the island worked in Brick, the clouds in Hungarian Ground and a border of Parisian. The footstool uses BNS design, Parisian background and side gussets in Bargello.

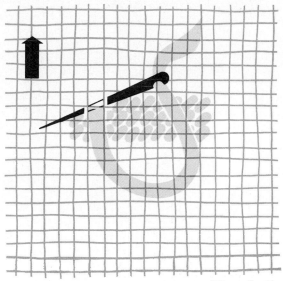

(Graph 6)

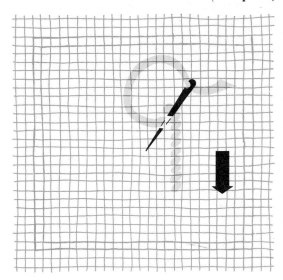

(Graph 7)

Emerge to the front of your canvas, right under your last End Hole, and repeat the process of working a BNS, emerging to the left of your Main Line Hole, working another BNS, and so on (graphs 5 and 6).

The Continental pattern can also be worked from top to bottom of your canvas. You have just learned how to work it from right to left. In working it from top to bottom, just reach *under* your Main Line Hole to emerge, work a BNS, reach under your Main Line Hole again, and so on. To reverse direction, turn the canvas upside down and start your new row by emerging next to your last *End* Hole, work your BNS, emerge under your Main Line Hole, and so on, and work down again *(graph 7)*. Very simple, really.

Keep in mind that a right-handed person must work the Continental from right to left or from top to bottom only, and that is why you have to keep turning your work upside down. When you have worked from right to left and want to head back, you *can't* unless you turn your canvas so that the left *becomes* right and you find yourself working from right to left again. The same thing holds true in working from top to bottom.

Now, in your corner square, in the diagonal half that has not yet been worked, pencil in two digits signifying the year. Then in the Continental, or catch-as-catch-can (which is simply an odd BNS, always the same little slanting stitch but done here or there without regard to pattern), work these digits in whatever color you choose.

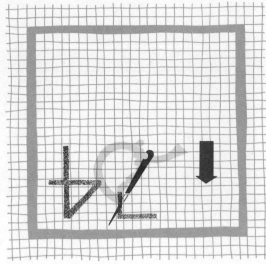

(Graph 8)

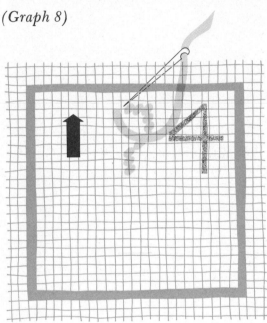

(Graph 9)

If I were working a seven, I would turn my canvas upside down and work the stem of the seven starting at the top *(graph 8)*. Here is a bit of confusion for you: when upside down, the *top* of the stem is really the *bottom* of the seven when it is right side up. *Right?* I would work the stem of the seven, and then when the last stitch was completed, I would turn the canvas right side up again, emerge to the left of my last End Hole (remember where that was when you were upside down?), and work the roof of the seven, moving to the left until it is done *(graph 9)*. Then weave the leftover yarn under the stitches at the back and snip off.

If I were doing a three *(graph 10)*, I would turn the canvas upside down and begin at the end of the curve (bedlam again—this is actually the bottom of the three when the canvas is right side up), work left and then down, turning right side up again when moving toward the center, and then upside down again to diagonal toward the roof of the three, and then right side up again to move left across the top. It can be a nuisance to keep changing the direction of the canvas, but the alternative is to have to make individual stitches, pulling your yarn through to the back each time. It is impossibly awkward for a right-hander to emerge in one motion when heading in the wrong direction. And pulling the yarn through with each stitch will slow you down intolerably once you are accustomed to the rapid smooth movement of continuous stitchery.

One more—a four. Start upside down and work the stem. Then turn right side up and diagonal down to the left, and then turn upside down again to work the cross bar to your left. On *graph 10* black arrows indicate stitches to be worked with canvas upside down, green arrows right side up.

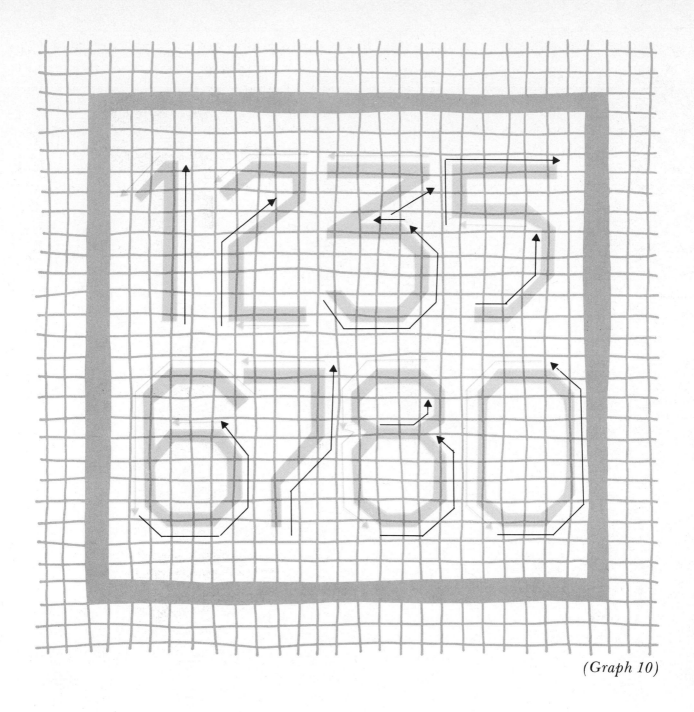

(Graph 10)

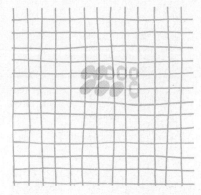

(Graph 11)

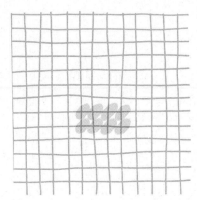

(Graph 12)

Experiment a bit outside the boundaries of your sampler if you feel unsure. *But,* and here I go repeating myself again but I know whereof I speak, just because a line is straight, as with a one, for instance, this does *not* mean that you suddenly lapse and work your stitches straight up and down (NOT THIS *graph 11,* BUT THIS *graph 12*). *No never!* You work a line of slanting basic needlepoint stitches one under the other, as in *graph 7.*

Have you noticed the elementary but important fact that whenever you emerge to start a new stitch directly under a Main Line Hole, your next stitch will be directly under the first? If you emerge *next* to a Main Line Hole, your second stitch will be next to your first. In other words, it is the Main Line Hole that determines where your stitch will be placed. The End Hole is always foreordained because you always have to slant up to the right. Yes, when I say slanting, I do mean slanting. Always.

When your digits are completed, work Basket-weave in any color you choose around them, starting in the upper right-hand corner. Your Basketweave pattern will be interrupted when you reach the digits, but just work around them as best you can. There is no cut and dried way to do this; just adjust as best you know how, moving up and down, always in diagonal rows, around the numbers. When the interruption is small, as with these numbers, you may weave your needle behind, and emerge on the other side of the digit, ready to continue the Basketweave pattern. When the interruption is large, simply reverse your direction as you did on the border of your sampler when you ran into one of your squares.

When your corner square is completed, select one initial from the graphed initial page. You will be using all your colors for this: one color for the background of your square, a second for the initial itself, a third for the stem of the flower, and a fourth and fifth for the flower. It is a colorful and lovely initial, graphed here for the first time.

Count the number of vertical and horizontal CATS that the letter covers from side to side and top to bottom and write it down. Take the S for instance. It covers nineteen vertical CATS from side to side and nineteen horizontal CATS from top to bottom. As our square is 24 by 24 canvas threads and we wish to center the initial as best we can, subtract the nineteen CATS from 24 and get five CATS, which means we will leave 3 CATS uncovered on the left side of the S and 2 on the right. Write that down so you remember. Now, for the top to bottom measure, 19 from 24 again leaves five CATS. We won't be able to center the S exactly, but the eye will not notice that. Just leave three CATS uncovered on top of the highest point of your S and two CATS uncovered below the lowest point. Now start counting those CATS; so many in, and so many down, and work your first BNS. Then stop and count again to be sure that you started in the proper Main Line Hole, having taken into consideration the direction in which your first stitch would have to move. Have you left the proper number of canvas threads uncovered above and to the right? If so, then begin your initial, following the graph.

Once again, use the Continental pattern as much as possible to work your initial, and when you can't use that, use the catch-as-catch-can filler stitches. Reverse your canvas as needed and be sure that you work from right to left or top to bottom. In that regard, it is probably advisable to begin each letter at the upper right-hand corner and work either down or to the left. With an H you would obviously work down. With an E you would obviously work to the left.

For the flowers, you may have to do a catch-as-catch-can stitch, as there is so little of any one color.

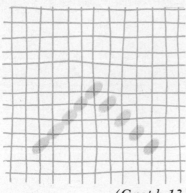

(Graph 13)

When your odd BNS stitches are close enough together, it is permissible to run your needle through some stitches at the back and emerge where the same color is wanted some distance away. But if your odd stitches of any one color are too far apart, that is, more than 1 inch, it is best to weave under, snip off, and begin again, rather than mat the back of your canvas with too much weaving.

When your initial is completed, work Basketweave around it, once again starting at the upper right-hand corner as you must always do.

You may notice that whenever you need a diagonal line, you can work your Basketweave configuration, as it will always form a perfect diagonal from upper left to lower right. As needlepoint is worked on squares, a diagonal from upper left to lower right proceeds down a step at a time, as you have seen with your Basketweave. But a diagonal line from upper right to lower left will not step at all, but will slide smoothly down (graph 13). Don't let this bother you; it's the nature of the craft. It's why circles are *never* really round—they just *look* round when they're finished!

LESSON
11

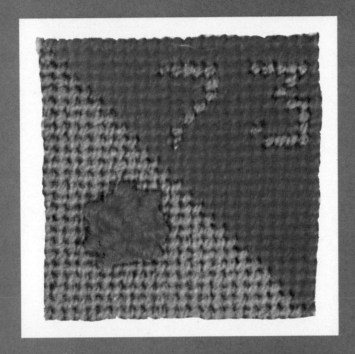

The
Whipped
Flower

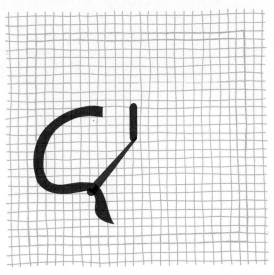

(Graph 1)

(Graph 2)

How to do the Whipped Flower

Your flower is superimposed on top of your Basketweave Stitches in your corner square. The upper diagonal half of that square contains the date. The lower diagonal half will contain the flower.

In the graphs I have used two colors, but when you work your sampler, use just one color yarn for both spokes and flower.

Select any color, three ply of Persian yarn, and emerge in the center of the lower half of the diagonal. It is not easy to find the center of a triangle, but come as close as you can. Following the graph (which for purposes of clarity does not indicate the Basketweave Stitch background) and use your yarn to construct six spokes of a wheel, always returning to the center after each spoke (graphs 1, 2). Try to make each spoke the same length if possible.

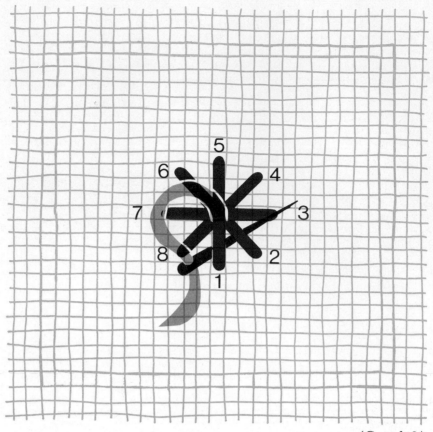

(Graph 3)

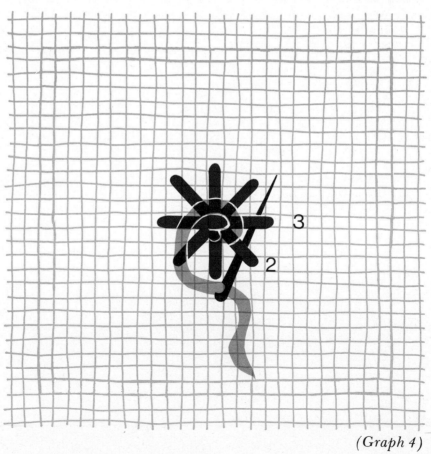

(Graph 4)

224

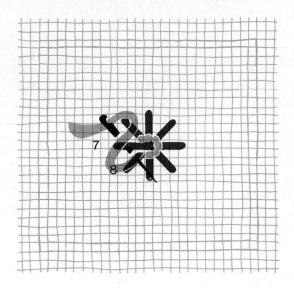

When this is completed, emerge near the center of your wheel. From this point on, your work is on the top surface of the canvas only. Dip your needle under two spokes (1 and 2) counterclockwise and pull your yarn through, pushing it toward the center of the wheel *(graph 3)*. Now dip back under spoke 2 continue under spoke 3 *(graph 4)*, pull your yarn through, and push it once more toward the center. Now dip back under spokes 3 and 4, next under 4 and 5, then under 5 and 6, and so on *(graphs 5, 6)*.

(Graph 5)

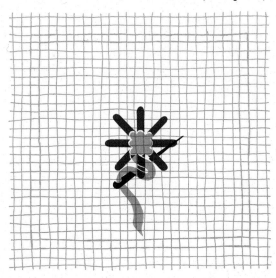

(Graph 6)

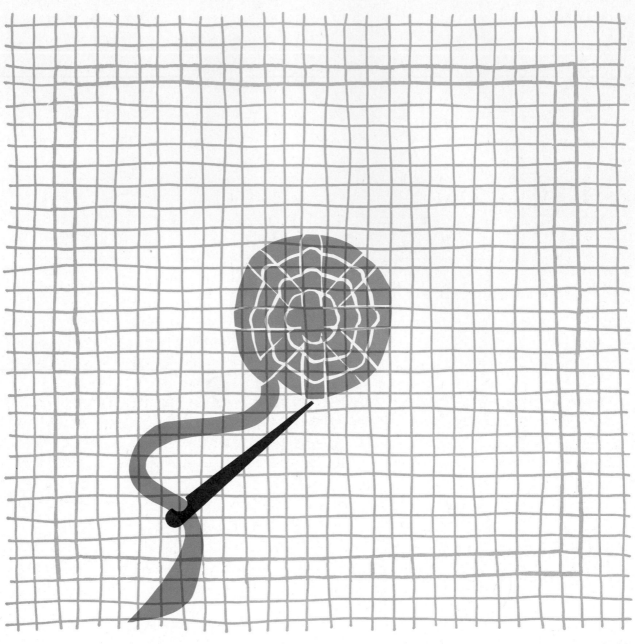

(Graph 7)

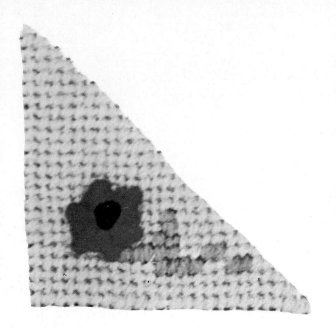

Turn your canvas as you dip under your spokes, and continue on in this manner until you cannot work any more, about three complete turns of the wheel. We want a nice full flower *(graph 7)*. If you run out of yarn while you are working, simply reach through to the back of your canvas and anchor your tail of yarn. With your new strand, weave under some stitches at the back and come up approximately where you left off. Continue whipping your flower. When it is completed, reach through to the back, weave your leftover yarn under a few stitches, and snip off. A French Knot, in a contrasting color, right in the center of your flower, is effective.

If you do not know how to make a French Knot, which is not needlepoint but belongs to the art of embroidery, here's how. Bring your needle up through the dead center of your flower. Before inserting your needle nearby in the center again, twist it twice around the main line strand close to the Main Line Hole, and insert. Don't pull your yarn through to the back too hard; pull just enough to leave a nice French Knot in the center of your flower. Weave your leftover yarn through the back and snip off.

Blocking and Deciding

Now that you have finished your sampler, it is ready for blocking. With a clean sponge, dampen it thoroughly with cool water on the reverse side, and then staple, right side down, to a piece of board or plywood. Pull it tightly into as square a shape as possible. Keep the staples near the edges of your canvas, a good distance from your stitchery in case they rust. Leave your sampler stretching in this manner until it is completely dry—usually about 48 hours.

When it is blocked, it is time to decide how best to show it off. If you decide it should be a pillow, it is best either to fill it with down or a filler that can go to the cleaners without worry (kapok might disintegrate when exposed to cleaning fluid), or fit it with a zipper so the outer cover can be removed. Your needlepoint can be cleaned or sponged down gently with soap and water.

You may prefer a knife-edged pillow, the easiest to make if you are to do the work yourself, plain or perhaps with four fat tassels (page 230) or fringed (page 47). A knife-edged pillow with piping frames your sampler beautifully (page 230) or perhaps you prefer a box-edged pillow (see page 213).

There are other decisions to be made if you decide on a pillow. If you plan to use it in a formal setting, a velvet backing is durable and lovely. Linen velvet doesn't have the subtle shading of some of the other velvets, but it is the sturdiest. Silk velvet is gorgeous, but fragile and expensive. Synthetic velvets or cotton velvets, treated with a spot-shed spray, offer an enormous range of colors and wear very well.

Perhaps you are planning to use your sampler in a less formal setting—a child's room,

This turn-of-the-century Richardsonian house uses all the stitches taught in our sampler.

Patience, skill, and beauty: pillows can be worked in favorite colors to enhance favorite rooms.

den, or library. Why not use a soft wool backing, or for a den, suede with four tassels, soft leather, or even fur. Unless you are a very experienced seamstress, I would suggest sending your sampler out to be mounted professionally if you are planning to use heavy materials.

If your sampler is to go in a very contemporary setting and you are game for anything, try backing your pillow with a wet-look vinyl, or even a silver vinyl.

If you have decided to hang your sampler on the wall, the frame you select would be determined by the room you plan to use it in. Simple strip frames are the best in that they do not take away from your work. I would use, depending on location, either a flat strip of stained distressed pine or maple or a flat stainless steel or aluminum frame.

Needlepoint is usually framed without glass and without a mat. However, should you decide to protect it with glass, I would suggest the non-glare type.

If you would like a tote bag, it is best to send your sampler to a leatherworker. Bamboo handles are lovely, but an over-the-shoulder leather strap would also be practical. The reverse side of your tote could be leather, but many of my students have made a second sampler for the reverse side. One of my more ambitious students worked a geometric pattern of smaller and smaller frames, using all her newly learned stitches, and this she used on the reverse side.

A chair seat or footstool upholstered with your sampler will give you a lifetime of use and satisfaction. But if by chance the

The various samplers adapt stylishly to tote bag, framed wall hanging, pillow, and footstool.

231

chair seat you wish to cover is larger than the sampler, you can handle this in either of two ways. One is to center your sampler in a larger piece of canvas and work a basic needlepoint stitch border around the outside so that it will fit. The other solution is to mount your sampler right into an appropriate piece of upholstery fabric— perhaps a velvet or other sturdy, solid-color fabric—and fit this into your chair seat. Remember that many of the stitches we used on this 12-mesh sampler are quite large and might get caught in a ring or buttons, so mount it on a piece of furniture that does not receive too much use or abuse.

Wherever you use it, I believe your sampler will not only serve as an instructive reference point for your stitches in later years, but it will bring you pleasure and pride whenever you see it.

I don't mean to sound ungenerous in saying that I do not think that you should give away this first sampler. It is an important reference for you, one that you should keep to remind you of how each stitch is done and how it looks when done, in a way that no book can. By having it to refer to, you are able to decide whether this or that stitch would be more suitable for this or that usage. It helps you in working the stitch and in compensating future works. I refer to mine often. Keep this one. Give the next away. And the next and the next. They make gifts of love as no others do.

The
Alphabet

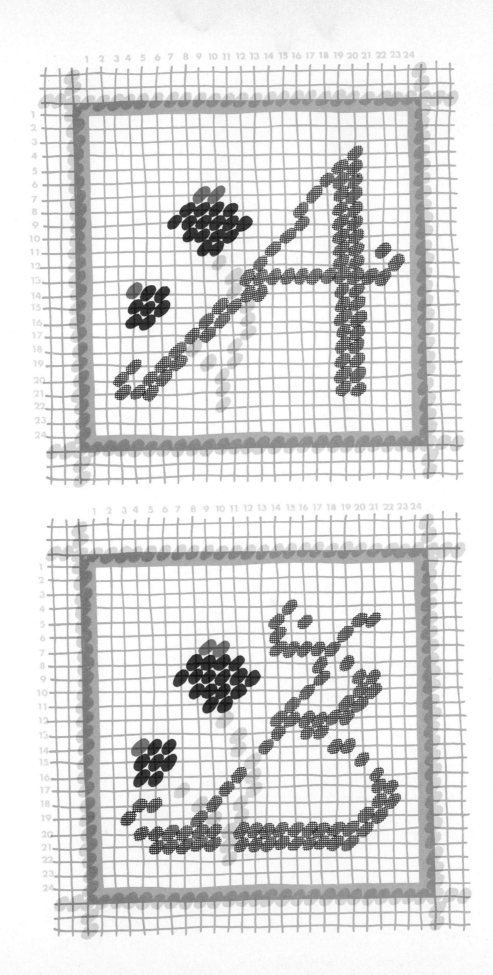

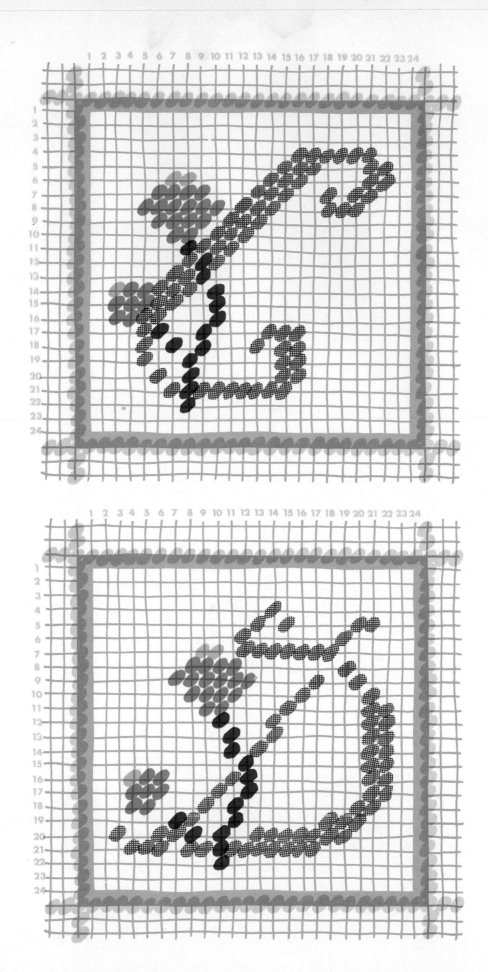

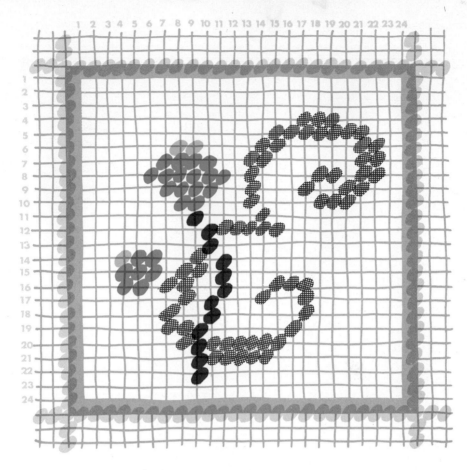

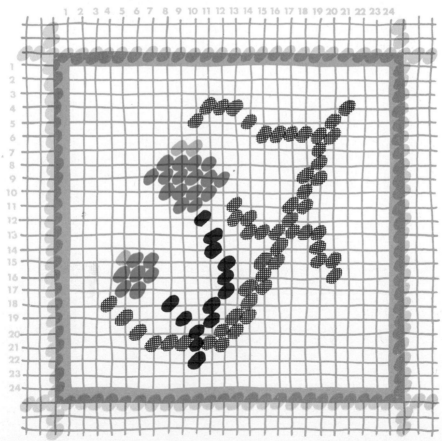

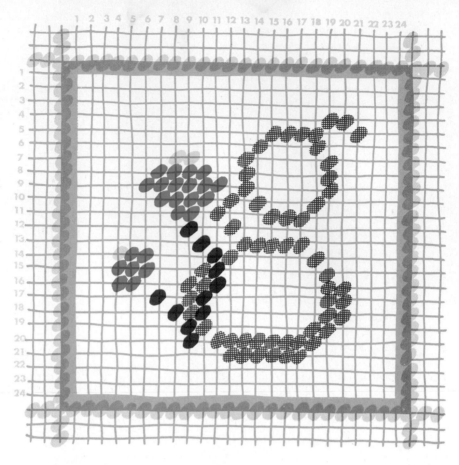

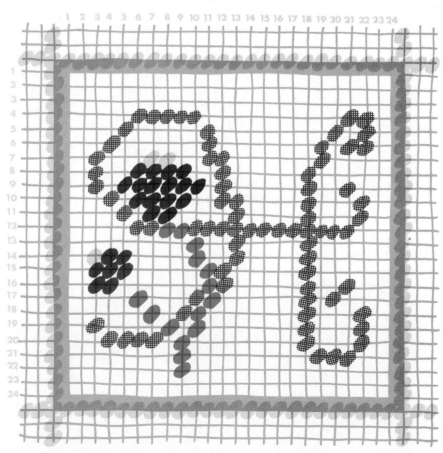

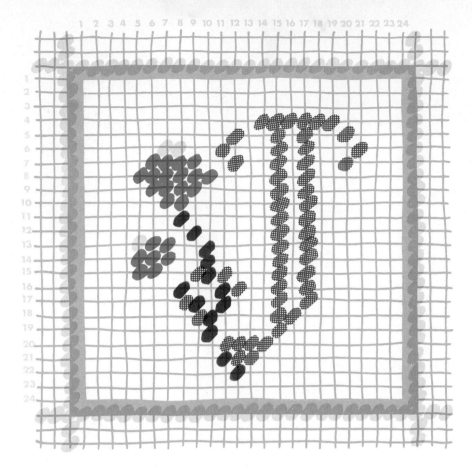

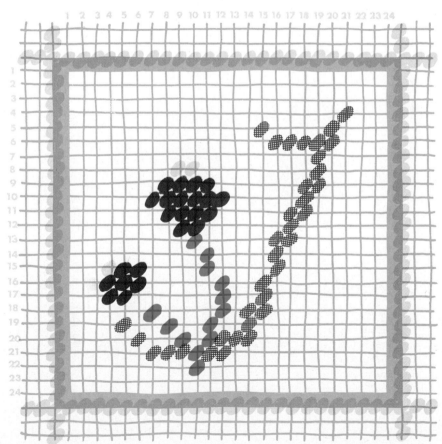

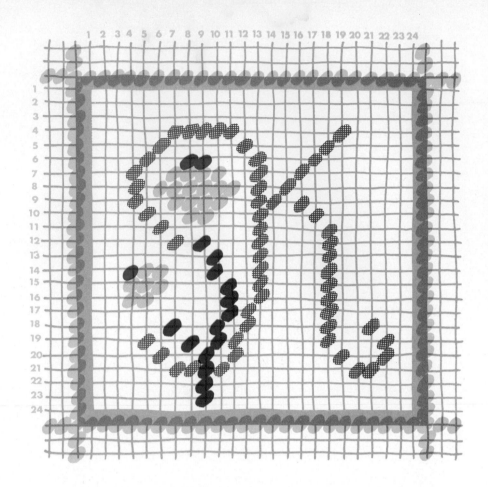

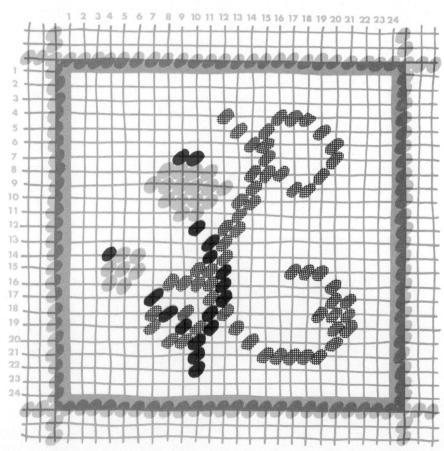

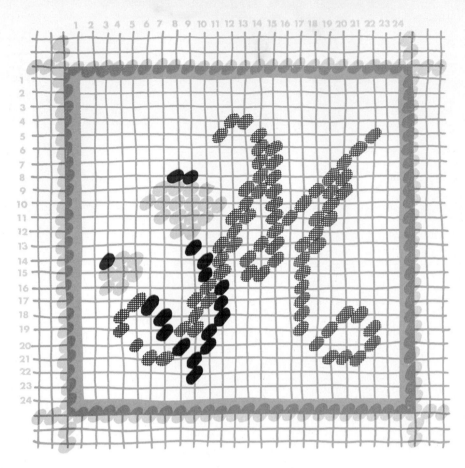

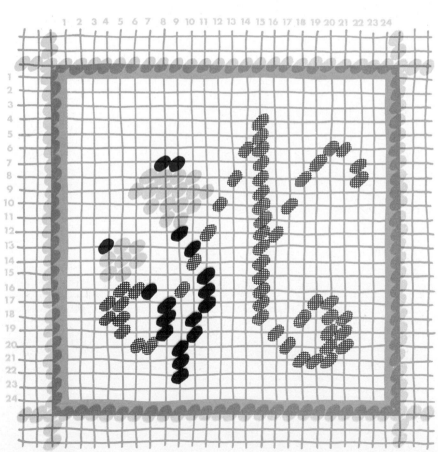

241

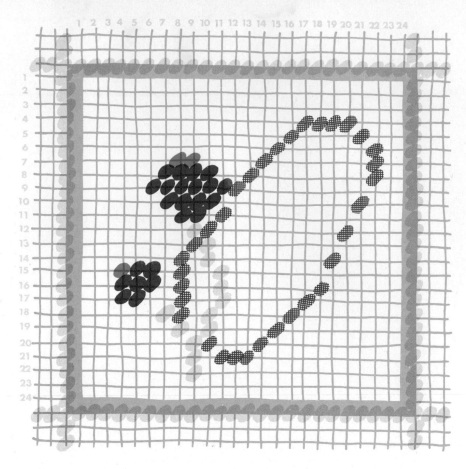

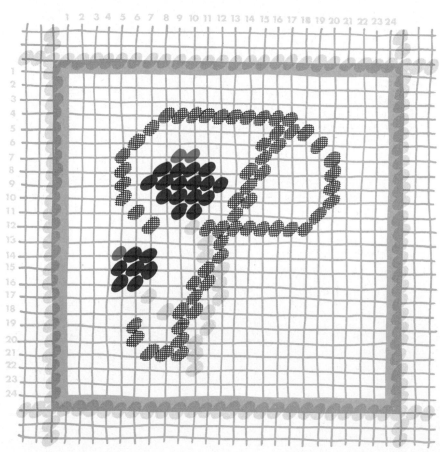

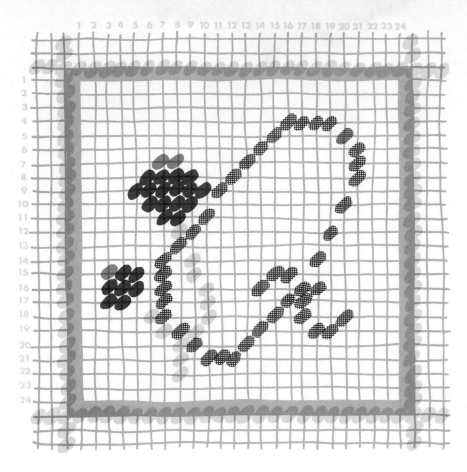

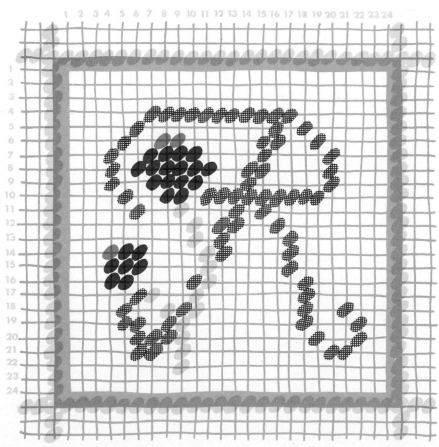

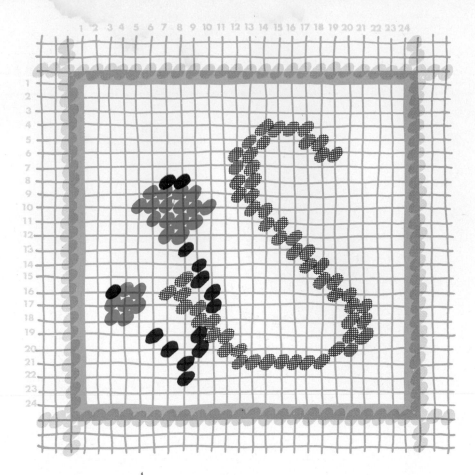

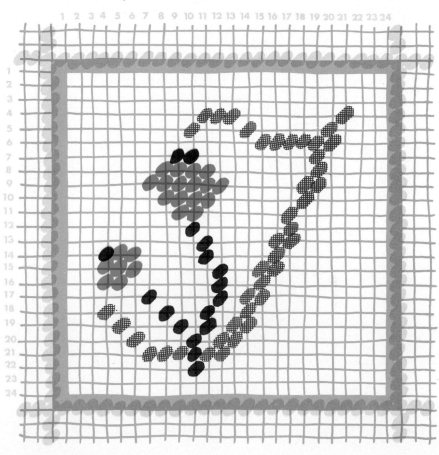

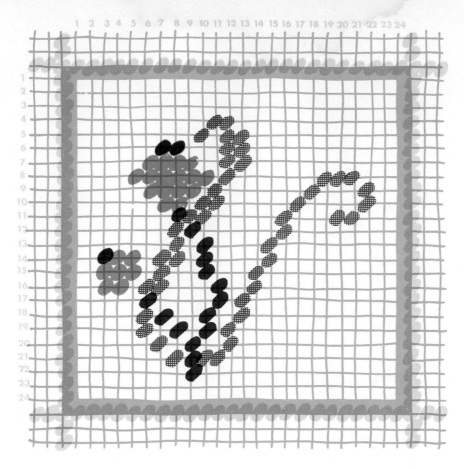

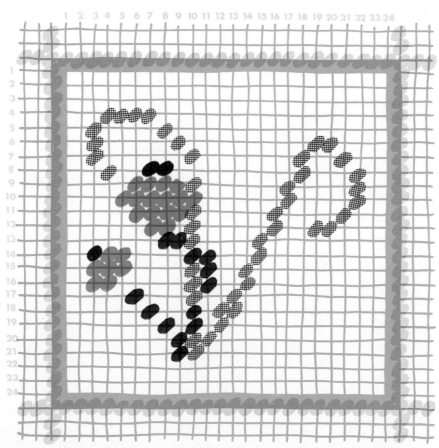

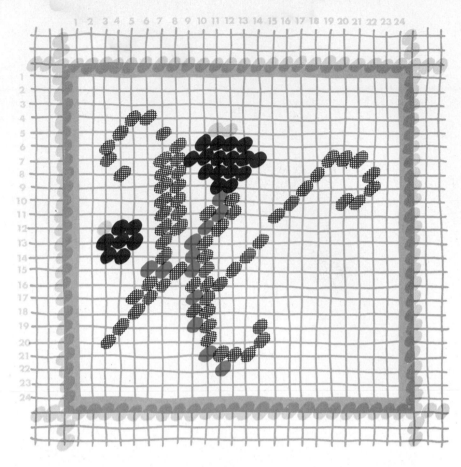

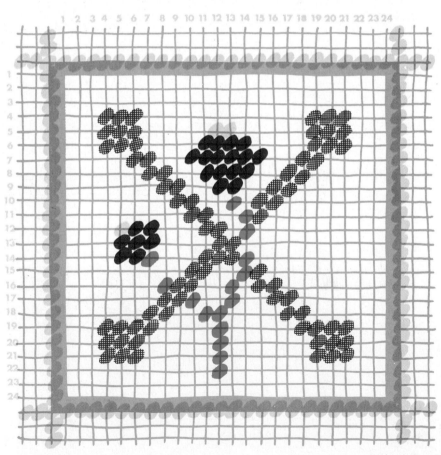

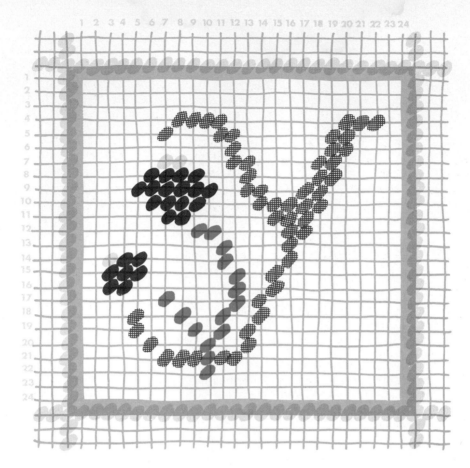

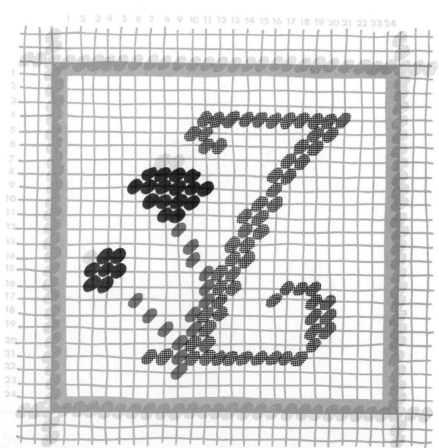

247

Shopping Information

Persian yarns and Persian type yarns are distributed or manufactured by the following wholesale concerns. If you write to them, they will inform you of the closest source to you carrying their yarns.

Paternayan Bros.
312 East 95th Street
New York, N.Y. 10028

Craft Yarns of Rhode Island, Inc.
603 Mineral Spring Ave.
Pawtucket, R.I. 02862

If you cannot find mono canvas in the shops near you, the following shop will ship anywhere in the world. It also carries sampler kits consisting of canvas already pencilled into squares with a variety of yarn color combinations. They also do all needlepoint mounting.

In Stitches
102 Yorkville Avenue
Toronto 5, Ontario, Canada